I0083058

RYAN WILMAX

SIMPLE ADVICE TO GET THE JOB YOU WANT

with Preparation and Job Hunting Tips including winning In Person or Remote (Virtual) Interviews and ideas to help Advance Your Career

W I L M A X

P U B L I S H I N G

First published by Wilmax Publishing 2022

Copyright © 2022 by Ryan Wilmax

All rights reserved. No part of this publication may be reproduced, stored or transmitted in any form or by any means, electronic, mechanical, photocopying, recording, scanning, or otherwise without written permission from the publisher. It is illegal to copy this book, post it to a website, or distribute it by any other means without permission.

Ryan Wilmax has no responsibility for the persistence or accuracy of URLs for external or third-party Internet Websites referred to in this publication and does not guarantee that any content on such Websites is, or will remain, accurate or appropriate.

Designations used by companies to distinguish their products are often claimed as trademarks. All brand names and product names used in this book and on its cover are trade names, service marks, trademarks and registered trademarks of their respective owners. The publishers and the book are not associated with any product or vendor mentioned in this book. None of the companies referenced within the book have endorsed the book.

Disclaimer

The author and publisher make no representation or warranties and disclaim any and all liability with respect to the accuracy, completeness, reliability, applicability, or fitness of the contents of this book. The publisher and the author are providing this book on an "as is" basis and do not make any guarantee or other promise as to any results that may be obtained. The information presented in this book is for educational purposes only and should not be construed as legal, financial, or tax advice. You assume the sole responsibility of relying on this information at your own risk. You should consult a professional to determine what is best for your individual needs. You are responsible for your own choices, actions, and results. Any names referenced in examples or stories are completely fictional.

For more information, contact RyanWilmax@gmail.com

First edition

ISBN: 979-8-9858600-0-9

This book was professionally typeset on Reedsy.
Find out more at reedsy.com

This book is dedicated to all of the teachers and mentors who invest their time to inspire others to improve themselves towards their passions and potentials.

"Far and away the best prize that life offers is the chance to work hard at work worth doing."

THEODORE ROOSEVELT (1858-1919)
26TH U.S. PRESIDENT
SYRACUSE, NEW YORK
SEPTEMBER 7, 1903

Contents

Introduction

If you are looking for a new job and feel a little bit lost or unprepared, you are definitely not alone. In a highly competitive job market, the difference between getting the job and not getting the job could come down to a few simple mistakes that may have been easily avoided. This book provides simple advice to help you get the job you really want by guiding your search, preparation, and actions to help you increase your odds of success while avoiding common mistakes. As remote work and online interviews are becoming more prevalent, knowing what to expect can help set you apart. While not every bit of advice may apply to your situation, perhaps just a few of the suggestions in this book could make enough of a difference to win the interview, get the job, and advance your career.

I

FINDING THE JOB

1

Knowing What You Want

Are you clear about what you want in your dream career? Some people want a career that allows work flexibility. Others want the highest paying salary with good benefits. And of course, everyone wants to work for a company that has great work-life balance and opportunities for advancement. However, it isn't enough to just list your needs and wants. You need to be able to discover, understand, and clearly communicate your goals and objectives to others. Knowing what you want helps you measure progress along your journey to keep you on track.

How do you set clear goals and objectives? Consider the following:

1. Goals. Identify what it is that you want specifically. For example, it isn't good enough to say, "I want to be rich." Be more specific and identify a target annual salary. Do you want to be a corporate executive? Try to be more specific by identifying a functional area, such as the Chief Technology Officer (CTO) of a company. Is there any particular company or particular industry that you want to target? What type of work do you enjoy or have a passion for? The more specific you can be at defining a goal, the easier it will be to develop a path to get there.
2. Reasons why. Know the reason why you want each goal. If you reached a particular goal, what would it really mean to you? How would it

change your life? Would being the CTO give you something specific? Do you want a specific job because it provides prestige, income, power, or leadership opportunities? What about reaching your goal gives you lasting satisfaction? What you need to identify is the reason why you want to reach your goals, which in turn, will motivate you to keep going each day. The reason why you are working towards your goal must be something that will make you happy.

3. Objectives. Identify the objectives you need to complete to get you to your goal. If you want to reach your goal of making $100,000 a year, what objectives can you take to get there? Do you need education or training first? If you are currently making $50,000 a year with promotional opportunities that simply won't get you to $100,000, perhaps you need to find a new type of job or a different employer that can enable you to achieve your goal. Make sure every goal you develop has clear objectives to get there. With each objective, give yourself a realistic time frame or deadline. Write them down. After you have those, see if each objective has any other smaller necessary steps or tasks. The more clarity you can document regarding your goals and objectives, the more realistic and more confident you can become as you complete each step.

4. Time frame. Do you have an idea of how long it will take to meet each objective? For example, if you don't have any computer systems experience, but you want to become the Chief Technology Officer of a company one day, you will need relevant Information Technology (IT) experience and training first to get there. Make the IT experience a short term objective and set a reasonable time frame. Once all of your objectives necessary to reach your goal are completed, you will be ready to seize an opportunity.

5. Review. Frequently reflect and re-evaluate your goals and objectives as you complete them. Make adjustments as needed. Keep a positive attitude when reflecting on past goals and whether you achieved what you intended or not. Never sabotage your future with negative thinking of what could have been. It will only hinder your ability to move forward.

Also, remember that it is not the outcome of events that is the most important to your life, but rather the quality of your decisions you made, based on the information you had at the time that counts.

6. Find a partner. It isn't enough to just write down a goal and then determine the objectives you need to achieve to get there. You have to stay engaged with the plan. One of the easiest ways to do this is to share your goals with someone else. It could be someone less experienced that can simply cheer you on, a coworker partner at your same level, or perhaps a more experienced mentor that can lead the way. Your cheerleader, partner, or mentor can help you periodically review progress. Many times, we won't share our goals with anyone because we are afraid we won't achieve them. This fear then becomes a reality. Don't fall into the trap. Instead, practice reviewing your goals with a partner because you and your goals are that important.

7. Celebrate your wins. If you don't have an accountability partner, you should find a way to reward yourself as you complete objectives that get you to your goal. For example, if you are in sales and looking to close six transactions in a month, you could challenge yourself by saying you will reward yourself with a nice dinner out when you have completed an objective to close three transactions. If you complete the entire goal of six transactions, perhaps you have a nice dinner and a night out with your family or friends. Never hesitate in rewarding good behavior or hitting key milestones that help you achieve your goals!

Whether it is career advancement or changing careers altogether, your positive "can do" attitude and focus will be your greatest traits. Be diligent and humble. This means you may have to take a step or two back before you can move forward. If you are an aircraft mechanic but want to become a Chief Technology Officer (CTO), you may have to first take a pay cut from making $90,000 to making only $60,000 as IT support for a larger technology company so you can gain necessary experience. This could be humbling and maybe you initially think that you can't afford the setback. However, try not to focus on short-term setbacks. Instead, focus on completion of the objectives necessary to achieve your goals.

The following is your opportunity to consider what you want, write down your goal, and outline the objectives and details necessary to help you achieve it. Take out some paper, a notebook, or an electronic device if you prefer, and document your answers to the following questions:

1. What do you want to accomplish, what is your **Goal**?

2. What are the **Reasons Why** you want to accomplish this goal?

3. What **Objectives** (necessary steps) do you need to complete to reach your goal?

4. What **Time Frame** is reasonable to achieve your objectives and overall goal?

5. How often will you **Review** your plan?

6. Do you have an accountability **Partner** that can support you in reviewing your plan and monitoring your progress?

7. What can you do to **Celebrate** achieving each objective and ultimately your goal?

Writing goals and taking the steps needed to get you there isn't always a simple process. It can take trial and error and a lot of practice to really understand and work through it. You may find that after really focusing on how to get there, you realize that your goal of making $100,000 per year isn't worth it. Perhaps you truly understand that what you really want is flexibility or work-life balance. Flexibility to have more free time away from work, time to travel, or spend even more quality time with your family. Maybe just having enough money so you can travel and not have to worry that your basic household bills are paid. There might be other ways to make that happen that don't include making $100,000 a year. The point is, don't get frustrated. Keep an open mind and know it is okay to redesign your goals. The chances are you will do this more than once!

Once you have taken the time to figure out what it is you really want and why, the goal planning exercise may bring you to the conclusion that you need to do more research to determine what it will take to get you to your goal. Consider training and education as a necessary and important part of the equation.

Educational Preparation

Statistics show that those with higher education tend to be compensated more in the work force. Data from the U.S. Bureau of Labor Statics, https://www. bls.gov/careeroutlook/2020/data-on-display/education-pays.htm, shows that not only does higher education increase earnings, but it also decreases the rate of unemployment. This doesn't mean that you can't be successful or be a high earner without a college degree. We all know some successful people that never finished college. However, their success likely had more to do with connections, support, or timing of their endeavors. Many of those individuals are the exceptions and not the norm. To give yourself the greatest chances for success, the more education you can obtain, the better.

A degree may not be the right choice to elevate your career. However, you should consider the types of jobs you want and look at the industry educational requirements. For example, some accounting firms may require a 4-year bachelor's degree in accounting. While some other positions may require the additional step of obtaining a state license as a Certified Public

Accountant. Know where you want to go and bring a strong work ethic. Ask questions, find mentors, research, and network.

You can research starting salaries of typical graduates from a particular educational program so you're not surprised when you graduate. This information can be found at the Bureau of Labor and Statistics, https://www.bls.gov/ooh/. You will also see projected growth of certain jobs and industries as well.

Research the advancement opportunities that are available to typical graduates. Reflect on if you could see yourself in this profession for the next 20 years. You want to be sure that the time, money and effort you invest will be worth it. If you can't see yourself in this career for the next 20 years, you may want to consider something else.

If a degree isn't required, sometimes professional training or professional certificates can help set you apart from others. Consider gaining additional certifications or training to give yourself an edge. Some certifications can be earned in less than a week for little to no cost. Other certifications may take weeks or months but could be well worth the effort. Not only will it make you look like a stronger candidate, you will likely learn something in a field you care about!

For promotions and upward mobility, most organizations will offer continued training and educational opportunities. Techniques, processes, and information systems are constantly changing, and you will need to keep up or you will be left behind. Many organizations offer tuition reimbursement or financial incentives for going back to school.

If you skipped college, didn't finish, or missed similar learning opportunities you wish you had completed in the past, remember it is never too late to go back to school or seek additional training to set yourself up to qualify for a new career. Regardless of the industry you pursue or the type of work you plan to do, having a student mindset, of humbly learning all you can, will serve you well. Consider education and training as a lifelong pursuit. Always be ready and willing to learn something new! One thing is always certain, and that is change. If you pursue goals that you are passionate about, you will enjoy the journey so much more.

Skills and Experience

Once you have identified your goals and considered objectives needed to accomplish them, ensure you consider professional skills and experience that will be needed as well. Do you have any abilities or skills that have remained untapped that you haven't had the chance to utilize? Reflect on skills you enjoy using, skills you would like to improve, and also consider new skills you have always wanted to acquire.

2

Preparing your Resumé and Cover Letter

Once you have a clearer vision of your future career goals, you may realize that you cannot meet these goals via your current position. A new job may be needed which, in turn, means preparing or updating your resumé. While you are working on it, the key is that you will need to tailor your resumé not to what your current experience or job is, but rather to the job you are seeking. You resumé should impress, but also be accurate. With this in mind, let's dive into how you can build a winning resumé designed to help you achieve your future goals!

Resumé Appearance is Important

Make your resumé visually appealing. A cluttered and disorganized resumé makes a resumé reader think that you, yourself, are cluttered and disorganized. If you are not the creative type, that's okay, your resumé doesn't need to be an art piece. The font should be consistent throughout using 12-point fonts that are professional and easy to read, like Times New Roman, Georgia, Calibri or Helvetica. Avoid visual elements that are distracting. If using a template, you can keep any text boxes or bullet points, but lose any distracting graphics. Multiple colors should also be avoided. Black and white should be the only colors with perhaps a third color for a few highlights. If you aren't sure how to format your resumé, start with one of the many great resumé templates out there that are simple and will help yours stand out. Canva.com has many free versions. Microsoft Word also has many resumé templates you can use.

Keep your resumé in a standard format that is concise, so it will be easy to update quickly. Here is an example:

Ashley Lynn Holiday

Cell: 555.555.5555 | gmail@gmail.com | New York, NY

Summary
Proven supply chain manager with experience collaborating at all levels of an organization to achieve cost reduction and quality goals. Excellent communication skills in creating productive and enduring partnerships. Pursuing a full time job in Supply Chain Management and Business Sustainability.

Personal Profile
Responsible, organized, determined, hardworking, creative.

Work Experience
Big Corporation   New York, NY   2020 – Present
Supply Chain Manager
- Responsible for 20+ vendor relationships
- Responsible for annual procurement of $2M in component parts
- Management of lead times for critical assemblies
- Inventory and capacity management and analysis
- Led supplier negotiations resulting in $500k in quarterly savings

Going Green Corporation   Los Angeles, CA   2017 – 2020
Business Sustainability Analyst
- Responsible for executing on strategy for business sustainability
- Ensure that products are sourced from sustainable areas
- Research and communicate latest in sustainable methods
- Saved $1.7M over three years

Education
Arizona State University   Tempe, AZ   2013 – 2017
B.S. Supply Chain Management and Business Sustainability
- Graduated May, 2017
- GPA 4.0
- Completed courses in Business Management, Accounting, Marketing, Purchasing Logistics, and Finance.

Skills
Microsoft Word, Excel, PowerPoint, Google Suite.

Awards Received
Employee of the Quarter, June 2020
Awarded Best Sustainability Project by Board of Directors

References
Available upon request

Keep it Simple!

Hiring managers are often looking at hundreds of resumés, so keep it simple! The elements of an effective resumé are:

1. Name and contact information. Never list, provide, or use your current work email during your job search. Instead, use a personal email address. Ensure the personal email address you will be using is professional. If the email address contains inappropriate words or connotations, simply create a new account. Be sure to check your incoming call voicemail message. If it sounds unprofessional, change it immediately. The last thing you want is to have someone call to schedule an interview and be put off by an unprofessional voicemail greeting.

2. Summary. This section describes your relevant qualifications and essentially who you are professionally. You can also include a sentence about what you are looking for, previously used in a resume section labeled "objective." Try to keep this section limited to three or four sentences. You may consider customizing this section depending on the job or industry you are pursuing.

3. Personal profile. Use some key adjectives that best describe your professional traits.

4. Work experience. List jobs, titles, companies, dates, and locations. Prepare a list of your job duties and accomplishments in bullet form that highlight what you did. Be impressive but accurate.

5. Education. List degrees, schools, dates, and locations. Don't include your GPA if it was below average. Do include key classes that you completed and could speak to that define the essence of your degree. Generally, don't list high schools unless you just recently graduated. If you don't have a degree, consider adding extra training or certifications that you have that could be relevant to the position instead.

6. Skills. List computer skills, academic skills, physical training skills, etc. Think of highlights in your skills or experience where you were recognized by someone or where you felt your best. Nothing is too small

if it is important to you or could translate to the new position, so take the time to brainstorm. If you lack professional experience, perhaps you taught yourself how to play the guitar. How can that translate? It can help show commitment to learning a new skill. The workplace has many opportunities to learn new things, and much of it is best learned if you have the right attitude and enthusiasm to teach yourself. Take the time to reflect on these types of skills and experiences so during an interview, you and a hiring manager can easily make a connection.

7. Awards. List achievements, special recognition, or anything you are proud to have accomplished.

Tailor your Resumé to the Job!

The goal of a resumé is to get an interview. With a visually appealing format, you can now showcase your summary, profile, work experience, education, skills, and awards received to the job you are applying. You may decide to customize the summary section to a specific type of job, company, or industry you are pursuing. You may also decide to customize it for one particular job you are applying. Carefully read the hiring manager's desired experience and skills and then craft your resumé to address those requirements. Further, check the company's website and social media. What you present on your resumé should mirror the company brand and culture so the reviewer can quickly determine that you would be a good fit for the company and position.

Many companies these days use software that analyzes keywords in resumes and compares those to content keywords in the job positing. It is beneficial to ensure your resume contains the keywords that are most commonly referenced in job postings that you might be applying for. Some applicants are even tailoring each resume to each specific job they are applying.

Maybe your goal is to change jobs and you want to go from being a host or hostess at a restaurant to working in a call center for IT support. You would want to think about the skills and experience at the restaurant that would translate well to call center support. Perhaps you took reservations over the phone and helped coordinate large personal and business dinner gatherings. How can this translate to call center support? These duties provided you the opportunity to develop good listening skills, coordinating with patience, informing the customer of various options, crafting creative and timely solutions that satisfied the customer, and communicating with key contacts as needs changed. All of these could help bridge the gap from one industry to the other.

What if you are an aircraft mechanic looking to change careers and move into technology? Mechanics know that if systems go offline, the safety of a plane in flight could be in jeopardy. What tools or experience do you have that may translate to preventing a company's network from going down? You could say that you work well under pressure. If so, this translates. Perhaps you could say that you are trained to follow complex instructions and protocols to ensure success. Be creative, but be honest. If you have skills and experience that may translate, showcase it!

If you are in doubt over your qualifications or feel the position you are applying for is a stretch, that's okay! It can be a good to stretch. With a little discomfort, we grow. Consider asking for feedback from those that know you best if you aren't sure. Figure out the skills you do have and how you could utilize them in a completely different field. Sometimes, it is the fresh perspective that hiring managers are looking for in a job applicant. And if you don't have all the direct skills applicable, engage your support system and use your references to help you determine the strengths that you already possess, as well as address any potential skill gaps, so you can more confidently determine the next steps that are best for your chosen career path.

Have References Available Upon Request

Pick who you use as a reference wisely. Don't pick a reference just because of their title as a doctor or CEO. It is better to have references that truly know you and have worked with you. Your reference can be considered an extension of you and therefore should represent you well.

References do not have to be your current or past supervisor. If you have a good relationship with them and they know you are looking, they could certainly be your best reference. However, a college professor, professional mentor, or colleague that knows your professional abilities could also make excellent references. Often, they are more than happy to help because they truly want to see you succeed.

Call and let your references know that you have shared their contact information with a hiring manager and that they may be contacted to be a reference for you. It is also helpful to say something like "I told the hiring manager that you and I worked on the office efficiency project together and won recognition for saving the company $10,000 over the course of six months." This way, your reference won't feel unprepared when they get a call and need to discuss some details of working with you.

If a recommendation letter is needed for a job application, ask a reference if it would be helpful for you to draft a recommendation letter, and then they can simply review, edit as needed, and sign. This way you can write the letter to highlight your skills, experience or traits that you feel best represent you for the position's needs. It also takes some time pressure off of your reviewer, since you have provided much of the background details, and they are now more enabled to simply focus on the feedback they'd like to provide.

Proofreading Matters!

One of the most important tasks you can do when hunting for a job is to proofread your resumé before sending it! You should triple check for spelling and grammatical errors. As you read, don't go too quickly by reading in your head what you *think* it says. Slowly read out loud the *actual* words that are there. This technique may help you find and eliminate errors that a reviewer would notice. Once you have proofread it, let it sit for a day or two before proofreading it again. After you are done reviewing, share your resumé with a few other people, preferably those that are detail-oriented, excellent readers, and ask them for any and all feedback. You might be surprised when offered ideas or suggestions that could make your resumé even better.

Your resumé is the first thing a recruiter or manager will see. Many applicants are never even given a chance for an interview due to poor spelling or grammar on their resumé. Too many spelling errors can easily lead to, "let's just throw this resumé in the garbage." Your resumé should represent your best work and the quality of work you will produce, if hired. Many times it is the very first impression a hiring manager will have of you. Make it your best!

More than a Cover Letter

The point of a cover letter is to draw interest and attention to your resumé which will, hopefully, get you an interview. While a resumé is a summary of your professional life, a cover letter is simply meant to introduce you in a more conversational way and encourage them to want to know more about you and how you would make a great addition to their team. Unless you have already been able to get an interview, sending a cover letter with your resumé is always preferred. Here is an example:

February 1, 2022

Mr. Mark Patterson
Human Resources Director
Large Corporation
10 World Way
Los Angeles, CA 90045

Dear Mr. Patterson,

My name is Ashley Holiday and I discovered the open position for a Supply Chain Manager listed on your company's website. I am presently working as a Supply Chain Manager at Big Corporation in New York and looking to relocate to the Los Angeles area. I am excited to discuss how my skills and experience in supply chain management could be utilized at Large Corporation.

The Supply Chain Manager position lists procurement of component parts as well as vendor relationship management. I have worked in a similar role with Big Corporation while also being responsible for management of lead times of critical assemblies. I am responsible, organized, and hard-working, traits well-suited for the Supply Chain Manager position. While at Big Corporation, I led a company project to complete a one year review of operations and completed it $200,000 under budget, and within only 8 months. The results of the project ultimately have saved the organization over $2 million to date.

Thank you for your consideration for this position. I'd like the opportunity to further discuss the position and my experience with you. May I have an interview? I can be contacted at gmail@gmail.com or at (555) 555-5555. I will contact your office on Friday to follow up.

Sincerely,

Ashley L. Holiday

Include the following items in your cover letter:

1. Date.
2. Hiring manager's name, title, company, and full mailing address.
3. Salutation.
4. Introduction. Write about who you are and how you found the job

posting, a little about your expertise, and why you are applying.

5. What you have to offer. Explain how your traits, skills, experience, personality or goals align with the job. Use information from the job description to form the bridge. How will you contribute to the company? Briefly highlight some recent accomplishments that are relevant. Use numbers to show specific results. For example, if you completed a multi million dollar project that was originally scheduled to be completed in one year, but you did it in only 8 months, make it known. If it was $200,000 under budget, even better.

6. Conclusion. Be sure to thank them for their time and consideration, include the easiest method to reach you (email, cell phone, etc.) and ask for an interview. Finally, it is wise to let them know you will follow up.

7. Closing. Add a closing, such as "Sincerely,"

8. Your Name. Type your name. You can insert your real signature above your typed name if you would like to add a more personal touch.

Once you have written your cover letter, consider how you deliver it along with your resumé. You could apply online, email it as an attachment, use regular mail, or perhaps the best method if possible, would be to stop by the office to drop it off. Creativity and hustle can give you an extra edge.

Unique Delivery

It never hurts to take an extra step when you really want to capture attention and interest. Consider personal delivery of your resumé and cover letter. A drive to the office and a courteous inquiry on whether the hiring manager is available could set you apart from the other applicants. If you choose to go this route, be sure you are dressed and ready for a potential on-the-spot meeting with decision makers. Dress up, you just might get an in-person interview!

Example: A young man had a hard time trying to get his first job after turning sixteen. He was given advice to write a resumé and cover letter, then put on a suit, and deliver these two items to a hiring manager in person. He wondered why he would need a resumé, cover letter, and suit if he was "just a kid" looking for an entry level position. He decided to follow the advice and wore a suit into three different restaurants to apply for open positions. He was offered jobs by all three on the spot. He reported back that he had two other friends apply for jobs at the same restaurants and they didn't get offers. He was able to choose the best offer from the three restaurants. His extra diligence paid off! Now, granted this example isn't the same as winning a vice president position at a bank, but preparation frequently leads to success. Taking the extra step to demonstrate initiative is never a bad idea.

Be creative, but keep it professional. The idea is to captivate so you can get an interview. Remember, if you are offered an interview, on the spot or at a later time, take it! Don't hesitate. You have nothing to lose by participating in an interview. An "on the spot" interview might sound intimidating, but just relax, breathe deep, and stay on point. Pretend that you're just going in to have a pleasant conversation. You should have already done research on the company to know your talking points. If you are offered an appointment for a later interview, maximize the opportunity to be even better prepared.

Always Update and Improve your Resumé and Cover Letter

Your resumé will grow and improve as you do. Frequently take the time to go back to add, modify, and remove information from your resumé so it is always current and the best representation of your professional qualifications. You never know when an opportunity will arise. You want to be able to respond quickly with an updated cover letter and resumé. Capitalize on opportunities that may come at any time. Be ready!

3

Remote Work Considerations

The Covid 19 global pandemic has reached and impacted every country and every community on earth. Many businesses closed office doors and shifted their operations from offices to employee homes. And while much of the business world has opened doors and brought back some office workers, there has been an awakening in both the workforce as well as corporate leadership in considering the costs, benefits, and various impacts of remote work. Both businesses and workers are seeing substantial benefits of remote work, enabled through recent advancements in technology. Many employees aren't ready to go back to the old normal.

Many corporations have reduced office space, utilities, business travel, in office perks and limited face-to-face large meetings and gatherings. The cost savings were staggering in some organizations. Companies big and small are considering completely remote work while others are offering some employees to choose hybrid work options. Of course some types of jobs require tasks to be completed in person, on-site, but many positions previously considered on-site only, have now been proven to be remote possible.

Employees have been introduced to the freedoms and benefits of remote work in other ways. Workers quickly learned they could save substantial amounts of time, money, and energy on commuting. They learned that wearing a suit and tie wasn't as important as simply getting the work done.

They enjoyed new found flexibility to start, stop and take breaks when needed. Working without office drama, gossip, and micromanagement has given a level of freedom that a majority of the workforce has never really experienced. And many now don't want to go back. As a matter of fact, workers are resigning their old jobs in droves. For millions of people, remote work is here to stay, and for some, is clearly preferable than going back to an office.

The pandemic has forced all workers to re-evaluate what is truly important. Confronted with our mortality, quality of life moved to the forefront and conversations regarding work-life balance turned from a trendy recruiting phrase to a more commonly understood way of professional life.

Now, if you haven't considered your thoughts on remote work, this might be the best opportunity. Does your goal include remote work or the option of remote work? Are you cut out for the remote work-from-home lifestyle or do you prefer the in person social interaction available in an office environment? Maybe you haven't been given the choice and now there are more options to choose from.

Remote work isn't going away. It will certainly grow and evolve in all industries and at all work levels. Remember that conversation about change and lifelong learning? If you can't envision remote work, you may have to narrow your job hunt to companies that support your preference. However, at this point for the foreseeable future, it might be easier to find a job that promotes remote work.

Some of the industries that have moved to remote or hybrid work options are:

1. Technology based jobs – Technical support, programming, developers, consulting
2. General office – Reception, administrative, human resources
3. Business administration & management – Leadership, executives, and middle managers throughout an organization (except for those in manufacturing, production, or construction). Some project managers
4. Professional services – Attorneys, accountants, consultants, insurance

agents, realtors

5. Call Ccnters – Customer service, support
6. Marketing and sales
7. Education and training – Teachers, professors, researchers, tutors

This is certainly not an all-inclusive list. What is important is to be sure to include remote work as part of your job search evaluation and conversation. Whether you want to work remotely or not, remote work is here to stay and you will want to know how to approach and evaluate the subject.

4

The Job Search

Before you begin your search, ensure you have determined what you really want in your job or career and laid out the objectives needed to reach your goal. You should also have updated your cover letter and resumé. Now, you have to determine where you are going to search for that new job or career. Where do you start?

It isn't always as easy as it seems, especially if you are trying to reinvent yourself. Of course, posting your resumé to job sites seems like a necessary and wise decision, but it isn't always the most effective. We're not saying you wouldn't get a job interview from these sites, but there can also be other approaches that can be successful. Let's explore all of your options!

First, consider if you want to work for a small business, large corporation, or government. Each will post jobs on different platforms, have different postings, interviewing and hiring processes, as well as different timelines. For example, many government jobs require a posting to be published for a specific time frame before closing the posting. Then, a rigid process of reviewers and interviews. However, small businesses are usually extremely flexible in their posting and timing for positions. It can be much easier as you generally communicate directly with an owner or hiring manager. Corporations are usually somewhere in the middle.

Let's compare in more detail some of the basic business types:

Small Business – The definition of a small business differs depending on what industry you are discussing. However, in general, a small business is considered one that is privately owned and usually has less revenue and employees than publicly held corporations. The size of the employee workforce can vary from 2 to 500 in the U.S. depending on the industry. To qualify for small business standing with the Small Business Administration, there must be less than 500 employees. Businesses from a "mom and pop" florist up to a local grocery store could be small businesses. Many small businesses are sole proprietorships, but they can also be legally structured as limited liability companies, partnerships, or even a corporation.

There are benefits to consider with a small business. Picking up the phone and asking for the hiring manager is a good approach to use if you are seeking a job in a small business. Often, there is a sense of community or family and everyone can get to know everyone else a little more. There is often the ability to have wide variety in your work duties or to easily move to other positions within the company. However, the downfall when working for a smaller business is there can be less opportunities for raises or promotions as well as difficulty in getting time off due to limited staff coverage.

Large Corporation – These organizations can be either privately or publicly owned. They do not qualify for Small Business Administration assistance or benefits due to their employee count or annual revenue. Examples of privately owned corporations are Cargill, Inc., and IKEA. Publicly held corporations can easily be found trading on a public stock market- such as Apple, Inc. (AAPL), Exxon Mobil Corporation (XOM), Honeywell International Inc. (HON), and Amazon.com, Inc. (AMZN).

The benefits of working for a large corporation is that they generally provide better pay than average, better benefit plans, opportunities for advancement, and relocation and pay increases. Many times there are opportunities to work in different specialties or departments as a worker's education, training, or interests change. Working for a larger company can generally provide more job security, but only if you are a better than average performer. If they have layoffs due to market or financial changes, sometimes there are opportunities to move to another department or position. Referrals and visiting their website job listings are good ways to discover open positions in a large corporation. However, large corporations can often be more ridged in their policies since they are managing thousands of employees. Workers can sometimes feel more like a number and less like an individual. Finally, corporations are generally more able to replace workers if performance isn't up to expectations since there are usually others available to take over a worker's tasks.

Government Work – Government positions can be for local, state or federal agencies. At the local level, you could consider city or county government jobs usually like community services and libraries, school districts, city parks, water and sanitation, police or sheriff's offices, fire departments, and many others. The state level usually has departments such as state universities, transportation (including motor vehicles), state parks, licensing and regulation, family services, statewide administration, etc. At the national level, you could consider hundreds of federal agencies in departments such as defense, education, treasury, commerce, justice, energy, health and human services, etc.

The benefits of working a government job is that once you are in, you can many times stay for your whole career if you choose to. Many jobs are stable and predictable. Most government jobs allow a wide range of mobility to other departments or agencies as opportunities arise. Some governmental entities still offer pensions to longtime workers, which can be a substantial financial benefit during your retirement years. Many government workers feel a sense of pride in their work as they feel they are supporting their community, state or nation, and providing a greatly needed service. As a result, some government workers enjoy a lifetime of fulfilling work. Referrals and visiting their website job listings are good ways to discover open positions in government. However, the downside to government jobs can be a lack of new opportunities and a lack of creativity or "out of the box" thinking since most processes have to conform to a myriad of legal and financial constraints and bureaucratic red tape. Also, some government agencies and employees have a reputation for a lack of motivation and therefore avoid doing any more than what is absolutely necessary.

It is worth evaluating whether a small business, large corporation or government agency aligns best with your goals and what you are looking for. However, keep in mind that these are all generalizations and while you feel a small business may fit more with your traits and desired work culture, you may find that a local school district has a culture similar to a small business. While you consider this information, make sure to keep an open mind as there can be great opportunities in all of these areas.

Job Search Websites

First, let's address job search, also called job hunting, websites. They can be helpful, and yes, you can get a job interview from them. And yes, you should post your resumé and even apply for jobs that interest you on these sites. The wider you cast your net, the better your chances. However, these sites aren't always your best resource. More importantly, job search websites should never be your only resource. Let's discuss how they work and who is using them.

There are numerous job search websites all over the internet. Perhaps hundreds or thousands by now. If you are going to use them, understand what you are aiming for. If you are a highly skilled professional or work in a specialized industry, you will want to focus on sites designed for those professions. However, if you are changing careers or looking in broad categories, you can span out to include more sites with general categories. Just keep in mind that sites that make it easy and convenient to apply have vast pools of other candidates also looking for a job. Also keep in mind that not all job search sites are created equal. Many of them will offer resumé building, hiring and interviewing tips, and other training. Some of the most well known websites are Indeed.com, Monster.com, CareerBuilder.com, ZipRecruiter.com, and GlassDoor.com. Because these sites are so popular, it seems that everyone has posted their resumé. Therefore, for popular jobs and categories, you may have much more competition for the open positions. If that is the case, make sure that the resumé you do post contains no spelling errors, is easy to read, and is concise. Be sure your profile is complete. Decision makers may look at your profile even before they ever get to your resumé! It may seem redundant because much of the information you put on your profile will also be on your resumé, but do it anyway. Further, since each site has their own system database, you will need to build and review a profile for each site. Frustrating, yes, but keep in mind that how you feel is most often how every job seeker also feels. If you complete your profile, you might put yourself ahead of the many others that didn't bother.

Consider going the extra mile offline. For example, if you post your resumé on a job search site, and then apply to a job listed, you might also think about calling the company directly and asking if you can speak with the hiring manager, a department manager, etc. Of course, this only works if the hiring company name is shown in the job listing. It is sometimes hidden to avoid this outside communication from job seekers. Regardless, the more proactive and resourceful you are in your search, the better your chances.

Another thing to consider is that not all employers use job search sites. Employers often have to pay for the service, and it simply isn't worth it to them. Perhaps they are large enough to have their own job listing database showing open positions, accessible through their website, and are able to easily find new workers. Consider visiting the company's website directly first, to see if the job posting is listed on their website, as it is usually better to apply directly if possible.

Sometimes not all job listings are listed directly by the employing company. Many are listed with agents or recruiters doing the hard work of filtering thousands of resumés looking for just the right candidate. This isn't necessarily bad, but just know that you are an additional step removed from the ultimate hiring decision maker. You are at the mercy of the website platform and the recruiter. Your message, what you have to offer, and what you are looking for, may not be as clear when there are more people between you and the decision maker.

Internship and Volunteer Work

If you have the time and the option to consider doing some work for free, consider an internship or volunteering for an organization that will help you make connections as well as offer an opportunity to gain skills and experience. There are so many worthy organizations that need help and would be grateful for your work contributions. You might be surprised that some internships or volunteer positions may compensate you. Even if they don't, they often hire from their internship or volunteer pool when a paid position opens up. After all, they trained you and already have worked with you, why not? Hiring from this pool is less expensive and time consuming for their organization and chances are better that you'll make a good addition to the employed staff.

If you want to consider paid or unpaid internships or volunteer work, a great place to start would be through your local school or college. Often, the career services center or alumni department can help connect you to companies and organizations that are looking for interns or volunteers. Another place to connect, if you have children, would be through your child's school. Joining the Parent Teachers Association (PTA) or helping in the library could lead to employment opportunities. Finally, consider your church or organizations that you have donated to in the community. Perhaps these offer an opportunity to start building your network to gain skills and experience. Making connections, wherever you can, could lead to an interview and then, perhaps to your next job. You can surely improve your chances and ultimately get better results!

Your Network is Your Lifeline

In 2020, the Bureau of Labor Statistics concluded that 85% of jobs were filled by networking. It would then be logical to conclude that if you were looking for a job, your network would be your first "go to" source to make an inquiry. People in your network can advocate for you since they already know, like, and trust you. When they start helping, like magic, their network becomes your network! However, it is not as simple as just letting your friends, family, and professional connections know you are looking for a new job. You need to follow up when recruiting your network for help and leads.

When approaching your network:

1. Identify people in your network. Business associates, coworkers, classmates, teachers, family, friends, and neighbors can all be considered as possible contacts to look for help. If your network is limited, look to join professional organizations or clubs that have frequent events. Consider both online and in person events. The more people and organizations you can associate with, the greater your chances.

2. Identify events and ways to connect. Large organizations many times participate in business conferences or tradeshows to showcase their products and services. Sometimes they are open to the public and have key company leaders in attendance. Some professional organizations host roundtable discussions or networking events. Various clubs host weekly meetings. Always be on the lookout. If you are invited to a luncheon, go! The best and most effective ways to connect are one on one opportunities. Having a quick discussion with a key individual beside their tradeshow booth can be much more informative than just reading their website. For more in depth conversational opportunities, you could schedule a lunch or just a coffee chat to gather more information.

3. Narrow your network list to key contacts. Try to identify any individuals that belong to organizations or companies that you are interested in. Perhaps they are in a particular industry that you are researching. Perhaps they have a specialized skillset that you'd like to learn or understand better. When interacting, always consider the idea that you are on a potential interview with those around you. If you are at a picnic and it is casual, maybe people are drinking, don't be the "party animal." Your next boss could be watching. Rather, take time to mingle and introduce yourself. Ask lots of questions. Work the room. Try to leave each person with something memorable. Sometimes it is helpful

if you can show you have something of value to offer. These individuals may help you identify your best leads. You will be surprised how often someone is willing to help you connect to someone else in their circle when you are considering new opportunities.

4. Actively engage. People naturally feel inclined to assist if you ask for help. But you have to do so in a tactful and non-aggressive manner. Don't simply tell everyone you are "looking for a job." Rather, be creative in your approach. Try to ask questions to understand their situation so you can better frame yours. Here are some sample questions:

a. "Which areas in your organization or industry are experiencing the most growth?"

b. "Do you have any advice for people trying to get into your industry or line of work?"

c. "Do you like working for your organization and why?"

d. "What is your company's culture like?"

e. "What is the best way to get more information about job opportunities with your company?"

5. Following up. When you follow up, be considerate. For example, if you call, first ask if they have a couple of minutes to chat. Always assume they are busy. If they do have time, remind them who you are and thank them for connecting. Be thoughtful with your interaction and try to keep it brief. Maybe you were having a good conversation that was previously interrupted and you wanted to ask a few more questions. If it would be helpful, ask if you could meet up again for coffee or a quick lunch when they are available. Always be polite and don't become a burden.

6. More following up. Don't just call a friend you haven't talked to in months and ask if he can find you a job in their company. Rather, reconnect with small talk and ask how they are doing. Explain that you are in transition and have researched the company they work for. Point out your area of interest and what you might be able to offer. Perhaps ask if they would introduce you to coworkers or the hiring manager. If the company isn't hiring at the moment, let them know that you would

still like to meet in the event that things change in the next few months. Ask if they are willing to be a reference for you. The main point is that you need to drive your job search, don't put it on them to do your work. If you show that you care about them, you have a better chance at finding good leads. If you really hit it off with someone because you have similar interests and career goals, ask to connect via social media or get their number to stay in touch. Then, follow up!

Social Media

Social media can be a double-edged sword when looking for a job or changing careers. It can be helpful or hurtful, so you must use it wisely. Before using any one of the social media platforms for job hunting or networking for a job, it is highly advised you remove any questionable, political, religious, or other controversial content that might be viewed in a negative light by others. Many companies, recruiters and hiring managers will scour your social media before a decision on hiring is made. If you question whether or not something should be taken down, just play it safe and take it down. Your years of education, planning, and job preparation could be easily wiped away by a bad impression from a controversial social media post.

Social media is a great tool to network, research companies, and find open positions. Community groups online will often have members who post that their company is hiring. There are also industry specific groups as well as business pages that are great resources to help you network your way into a new position.

If you do make an inquiry through a social media platform, make sure to keep it professional and positive. Make it easy to access your resumé and contact information. Follow up and keep in contact. You never know when a position will open up or you will connect with the right person at the right time.

It goes without saying that networking with those you know is the most successful option, but there are other ways to network as well.

Job Placement Agencies and Recruiters

You may also consider networking with job placement agencies and recruiters depending on the industry. Many companies will hire through these organizations first. There are even recruiters and agencies that specialize in placing temporary workers at large companies before making a hire permanent.

Many government jobs begin as contract jobs that may have an opportunity to transition to a permanent position. Other industries that will outsource jobs are IT, industrial, healthcare, professional, managerial, and general office positions. By offering and accepting a temporary position, both the employer and the new employee can determine if the company and position is a good fit before each side commits.

Keep in mind that these temporary jobs may not pay as well in the beginning, but often, if you are considered for a permanent position, the pay will likely increase.

Go Direct

Another great place to search for that next job is going directly to the source. Of course, don't try to wear a fake uniform and deliver a pizza just to bypass a security guard in the hopes you can catch a hiring manager. This only works in movies. However, there are many companies that you can just walk in and ask to speak to a manager if they are available for a few minutes. This approach works very well for many small businesses.

It is highly advised that you do at least some basic research on the company beforehand. Be humble, friendly, and patient. If the manager will see you, but they are in a meeting at the present time, ask if you can wait. Meanwhile, strike up a quick and courteous conversation with the receptionist, without trying to disrupt their work. Ask questions, gather intelligence, and keep it light. A receptionist is more than just a gatekeeper. They usually have the tips, tricks, gossip, and details to everything important. If you can find a way to make friends with them, you might make getting a job there easier!

5

Researching the Company

Networking and research go hand in hand. If you are looking for a new career or just a different job, do your research. You should know from Chapter 1 that knowing what you want is crucial. You should know the reason why you are pursuing this career, industry, job, or particular company. When you go into an interview, many times this is the first question they ask.

Why Here

Some people join the military out of a sense of patriotic duty. Some people become nurses or doctors because they want to really help people. It isn't always driven by money. However, going into a career blind to the typical educational costs needed or salaries being offered is foolish. Consider everything. Perhaps you want to work in Information Technology (IT). Is it because of the creative working environment? Is it because it pays well and has great benefits? Do you find the work challenging and want to be surrounded by like-minded individuals? Try to really understand why you are choosing a particular career, industry, or company.

When you are considering why you want to be a part of a particular industry or company, be sure to research whether or not your goal fits into the company's big picture. Do your goals complement each other? Does your "reason why" add value or contribute to the company culture or goals? How do you know? Be ready to articulate it!

Company Intel

You won't know how you fit in or what contributions you can make unless you do at least some basic research on the company. Review the company website and information about their senior leadership while reviewing the company's mission, vision, and values. Discover more about their main products and services and, more importantly, their new products and services. Take the time to find out about the company's history and culture. If they are publicly held, review their latest annual report. Also, spend some time doing an internet search for recent news related to or about the company. It may be helpful to see how others in the community view the company.

Common questions to address:

1. How are they different from their competitors?
2. What are the advantages or disadvantages of their products?
3. Are they considered better or worse overall?
4. If they are the best, how can you contribute to keep them on top?
5. If they aren't the best, what can you bring to the table to help them improve?

Maybe you have ideas on cost savings or efficiency. Perhaps you want to work on the leading edge and have experience in new technology. Perhaps you just graduated with a degree in supply chain management and believe you have ideas to help them source materials more efficiently or more sustainably.

When researching, think of yourself as a missing piece to a larger puzzle and consider how you fit it. Craft a story that shows you have taken the time to really research why you are a good fit and what you can contribute. Dig deep and take your time using all the tools available to you. You can start by doing some social media sleuthing!

Social Media in Reverse

While hiring managers and recruiters are scouring your social media, you should be doing the same. You can do searches for the company and for people who work at the company. Do a search for people and posts related to the company. You might be surprised what you can learn. Social media is usually in real time and some of the freshest data available, whereas news articles can be stale or outdated. When you review social media, keep in mind that certain information usually sits on different platforms. Consider these sites:

1. Facebook. Think of this platform as the family BBQ. Posts are more casual and often centered around recent or upcoming events such as holidays, vacations, reunions, promotions, new arrivals, etc. Comments can move from one thing to another, with people coming in and out. The information posted is usually tame and includes all age groups as most everyone is connected to everyone else in some way. Some companies also have Facebook pages with helpful, additional content.
2. Instagram and Twitter. Think of these platforms as the nightclub or local bar. Lots of random short conversations sometimes with strangers from all over the place. Usually, posts are for a younger crowd with some peacocking and showing off. A little loud, it's hard to keep up with people entering and exiting. However, some companies do have unique content on Instagram, even if it is a little bit trendier. Some companies use Twitter for frequent news releases or updates.
3. LinkedIn. This is more of the professional conference. You usually will find posts that discuss industry standards, changing professions, career training, news, etc. Everyone is on their best behavior and usually careful in what they post or share. This is not really the place people post about their kids or pets.

There is value in checking many platforms, but at a minimum, you should be looking at Facebook and LinkedIn. Think of it as attending the work conference and going to the company BBQ. You can get intel from both!

Now, it is worth noting that not all companies utilize social media due to various reasons. The healthcare industry has to be very careful and calculated in what they post, and their social media is highly regulated, needing internal and possibly external approvals for posts. Multiple reviewers are also often needed with government agencies and larger corporations. But it's still worth checking, since employees are more apt to share stories that may be helpful. It is all about digging for that golden nugget that will give you understanding or information that can set you apart.

Talk To People

One of the most efficient ways to learn about a company, their culture, what they do best and what they fall flat on, is to talk to people that currently work there. Better still, is to talk to people that recently left there. Facebook and LinkedIn both offer tools to send messages, so consider it.

However, you need to do this carefully since you are likely reaching out to strangers. Introduce yourself and then briefly explain the reason for messaging them. Have a few short questions to ask and don't waste their time. Be courtesy and cognizant of the fact that they do not know you and might be hesitant. Here is an example of how to approach someone:

> "Hello, my name is Ashley. I hope you are doing well. I am reaching out to you as I noticed you work for Large Corporation. I am considering applying for a Supply Chain Manager position and hope you might have time to tell me a little bit about the company culture from your perspective, how you like working there, or anything that might be helpful in preparing for an interview. I'd appreciate your thoughts. Thanks!"

Online Forums

There are several places to gain employee perspectives about a company. A great place to gather feedback from current and past employees would be to read online forums. As with any forum, you should keep in mind that much of what you read tends to be just the strong negative opinions. This is due to the simple fact that people are more likely to go out of their way to voice a complaint rather than a compliment. Therefore, be sure when using forums that you consider the reviews could be coming from disgruntled employees. This isn't to say that they don't have a grievance, only that you should place one or several reviews in context. Does the narrative make sense in light of recent changes in management or processes? Are the reviews recent? Do many different reviews seem to be consistent? If you find that the reviews are recent, consistent, and fit a narrative with a recent company-wide change, then you should consider that information and determine whether or not the reviews are a red flag or present an opportunity.

One online forum that offers a large database on company reviews is Glassdoor.com. You can easily input a company name and location and read reviews. You can also review salaries, jobs, and the company ratings over the past several years. While Glassdoor.com is one of the most recognized, there certainly are other sites to consider such as Vault.com, Careerbliss.com, and Comparably.com. Even some of the job hunting sites such as Monster.com include company profiles and reviews.

As a job seeker, you want transparency. You want to know more than what the job description says. You want answers to understand what it's *really* like to work for a particular company. These online forums and reviews can give a window into the culture, job satisfaction, and much more. Further, you can use these employee reviews of a company to frame your questions once you have secured an interview.

You will want to be specific with your questions and remain impartial with your tone, so you don't cause offense if the review or information is negative. Be sure you gauge how the interviewer responds. If they are truly honest and transparent, they will address your question directly. If they deflect or get defensive, you may consider this to be a red flag.

On the other hand, if a review is positive, be sure to mention it! Be specific, name drop the author, and perhaps they will get kudos. If you bring up a very specific review, it helps show that you have done your research and are already invested in the company. For example, you read a review that says the company has a very liberal leave package and one of the highest rated compensation packages. You could say, "I noticed several reviews on Glassdoor.com. Employees seem very happy with the compensation and benefits here." Conversely, you may have read several reviews that claim the company suffers from cronyism. You could say, "I noticed several reviews on Glassdoor.com that mention dissatisfaction with the advancement and promotions process. Can you help me better understand the process for advancement?"

Calculated Research

Keep in mind that your research is for a purpose. Sure, it's fun to find the gossip or funny photos. However, you really are looking for information to help drive home that you are the one they need. You are looking for current and relevant stories to tie yourself, your experience, and your skills to. If you find that they have launched a new product or started using a new process, find a way to incorporate that into your resumé or interview. Maybe they just brought on a new CEO with a new vision or opened a new division focusing on a breakthrough technology. What about their annual report? Did they acquire a new company, or did they just miss their financial targets? How can you fit into a positive narrative to help you stand out?

You make it easier for an interviewer to justify that you should get the job by showing you already have a plan on how to participate in solving a problem or contributing to a positive upward movement of their organization.

Here are some things to look for and consider incorporating into your job interview pitch:

1. The Company's Annual Report
   a. What were their financial goals and did they meet or exceed them?
   b. What were the major contributing factors to their financial results?
   c. What new products or services are they pushing going forward?

    d. How can you contribute to their continued growth?

2. The Company's Mission

    a. Summarizing in your own words, what is their mission statement?

    b. How do your skills, experience, or desire align with their mission?

3. The Company's Strengths and Weaknesses

    a. What does the company really excel at?

    b. What areas does the company struggle with?

    c. Who is their closest and strongest competition?

    d. How can your skills or experience help them perform better than their competition?

This may seem like over thinking and over preparing, and possibly for nothing. However, remember that attitude is everything! If you put some work in up front, it will make the conversations smoother and will surely be noticed. Most people will not go to great lengths to outshine other candidates when it comes to research. However, it can make all the difference in getting the job you really want!

II

GETTING THE JOB

6

Interviewing Basics

An interview is first and foremost an opportunity for a company representative to get to know you better and determine if your skills and experience meet the needs of their open position. However, the interview process is also an opportunity for you to determine if the position and company are a good fit for you. A good fit not only for your current needs, but your longer-term career goals.

You have the opportunity to influence the outcome. You have already analyzed what it is you want and you have done your research about this company. You are prepared to present yourself in the best possible light. Be ready to demonstrate your commitment, knowledge, and eagerness. The interview is your time to shine and you are in the spotlight. You have prepared for this moment and got your foot in the door. You have organized, researched, and planned. Now you can put everything into action. To stand out and make a great impression, follow these tips:

Be On Time

One of the simplest and most important, but most overlooked courtesies, is being on time for your interview. If you are running late, always call *before* you are late and apologize. After 15 minutes of being late, your chances of impressing your interviewer have vanished.

Show up early, fifteen minutes early. It's okay for you to sit and wait. It is not okay to get stuck in traffic and make the interviewer wait. Sitting and waiting gives you time to shift your mindset and settle your nerves. You want to be humble and grateful. Stay calm. Set yourself up to hit a home run.

There is nothing worse than being nervous and then being late with no time to recover. What about weather? Is it going to rain or snow the day of your interview? Are you taking public transit to get there? What hurdles could cause a delay? Consider what type of interview you are doing and then plan ahead. If you need to drive somewhere, you should research your driving route. Consider using a map application like Google Maps or Waze a few days before the interview and watch timing and traffic on this route. You may notice that in the early morning, it takes 20 minutes longer to get to your destination than it does mid-morning. Or worse, you may notice that a certain area of the route is prone to accidents. Plan for it!

If you aren't driving or commuting to your interview, there could be other considerations. An online interview still needs prep time as previously discussed. Any small or unexpected issue could not only impact your timing, but more importantly, your attitude. You can't account for every scenario, but you can plan ahead and avoid much of what could prevent you from presenting your best self.

If you notice your interview is running over the allotted time, ask if it is okay to continue. Never try to cut an interview short if you don't absolutely have to. If you have already made up your mind that you are no longer interested in the position, exit gracefully and politely. Going long on an interview is a fantastic sign that both you and the interviewer are forming a good bond and your chances of a second interview or an offer are high.

Attitude

The interview is a continuation of the story you have built up to now. For your first impression, attitude is everything. When you go into your interview, be confident but not cocky. Be optimistic, but not too dreamy. You want to have a memorable and strong presence in a good way. Be prepared for a firm handshake or perhaps an anti-Covid first-bump. Smile and share a simple pleasantry right off the starting line. A simple, "Hello, thank you for taking the time to meet with me. How are you doing?" can go a long way.

Be sure to avoid framing answers or giving narratives in the negative. For example, if you are asked why you left your previous employer, avoid saying things like the company was disorganized or the manager wasn't fair, etc. Without lying, frame a response giving an answer that is true without blaming. You could say that you believe you outgrew the position and didn't feel there was an appropriate path to advancement, or you decided you were ready for new challenges. Keep with "I" statements. This helps avoid finger pointing and keeps the focus on you. Even if someone at your former employer is a big reason you left, don't fall down that rabbit hole. Put your departure in the best light and make it a positive story about you and your future career, never a negative story about someone else.

Know What You Want

Most often, an interviewer will ask some variation of what it is you are looking for. They may ask, "Why do you want to work for our company?" They may ask, "Where do you see yourself in 3 to 5 years?" They most definitely will want to know what skills and experience you can bring to the company. Through your goals exercise and research, you should already know how you can approach these questions, but it is always good to practice beforehand.

Do you want challenging work? Are you looking to work for a company that offers advancement and training? Knowing and communicating what you want clearly will help the interviewer understand your values and goals better. The more cohesive and compelling your answers, the better your chances of standing out from other candidates.

Remember Your Goals

Whether it is salary, benefits or duties – keep your goals in focus. Perhaps salary for this next job isn't as important as advancement or flexibility. If the position is offering greater flexibility, you might consider taking a lower starting salary. However, if income was of greater importance, perhaps you can negotiate a pay raise after a ninety day or six-month review. There are many ways to work through details that will both benefit you and your future employer. Align your goals with the company goals and then articulate both, and you will have better success!

Know Your Worth

If you have communicated what you want and helped build a bridge between what the company needs and what you have to offer, then you have laid the foundation to discuss your value and expected compensation. It usually helps to research what the going pay range is for the position, as well as similar positions in other companies. Hopefully the job posting gave an idea of the pay range for the position, but if it didn't, now is the time to ask. It is worth noting that many companies will automatically start a new hire at the bottom of the pay range for the position leaving room for raises in future years. Some companies have already decided a specific dollar amount they are willing to pay and won't negotiate it. The current market environment, your desire to join this specific company versus others, and your personal threshold for salary versus other job benefits such as location, brand recognition, future advancement opportunities, etc. is part of the evaluation you must do to decide if this position is the right fit for you.

Are you okay with the salary or hourly wage being offered? Perhaps, but what if you are bringing significant additional knowledge or experience to the table over other candidates? Know what your knowledge and experience are worth, and what you are willing to accept. If you can articulate your value and why you are worth the additional compensation, you could possibly change the conversation in your favor and provide a compelling reason for them to pay more. It is helpful to know how you compare to the job's minimum requirements or other candidates. Anything you can demonstrate that is in addition to those comparisons could provide support for higher pay.

Negotiate

When it comes to discussing and negotiating salary, you should always attempt to negotiate their first offer. You could politely ask, "Is the salary negotiable?" or "Is there any flexibility in the salary?" You don't want to come off as difficult, but it never hurts to ask the question. Providing calm and thoughtful support for why you think you should be at the higher end of the pay range rather than the lower end is always recommended. If you were paid more in prior positions, simply say so. Providing information on prior salary or bonuses received from prior employers can many times help them support or grant your request. If a salary is low and not negotiable, explain that you had hoped for more but understand if that is all they can pay. Keep a positive and confident attitude, but be gracious. Some companies have pre-authorized a specific salary for the position and the interviewer doesn't have the authority to change that on the spot. This is where you have to know what you want and what you're willing to accept. Decide if this is where you need to part ways and keep looking, continue to try to negotiate other items, or potentially give in and accept their offer. If you think it best to keep negotiating, asking for additional paid vacation days is typically a common area of flexibility that employers can add to your offer to make it more attractive. Keep the conversation friendly and professional. If you feel uncomfortable accepting right away, you can always ask for more time to consider their offer.

If you are the top candidate, there is a chance they will fight to get you a higher salary, offer pay raises sooner, adjust bonuses, benefits or job duties that fit more in line with your skills, abilities, and goals. Focus on the facts, support for your reasons, and then make a decision to accept their offer or politely decline and keep looking.

Appearance

You will want to give considerable thought to your physical appearance. Interviews are all about presentation, and you can never be over dressed.

Your appearance should mirror the company image. If you are interviewing at a well-respected and highly visible law or accounting firm, full formal business attire is the way to go.

Formal business attire consists of matching two-piece suits in black, dark blue, or gray. Ties, hose and dark dress shoes are expected. Formal business attire should be dry cleaned and pressed (ironed). Casual business attire is slacks, khakis or dresses, basically allowing for more freedom. With casual business attire, jackets and ties are not expected. A nice shirt with collar, a blouse, or a sweater, can be considered acceptable. If in doubt, dress up more.

Usually for job interviews, wearing formal business attire is safer than casual business attire. If everyone is casual and you show up in a business suit, it's ok, you can never be over dressed for a job interview. However, in the reverse scenario, if everyone is wearing formal attire and you show up in casual attire, not only will you look out of place, you will look unprepared and unqualified for the position.

For women, avoid sleeveless shirts and flashy outfits. Don't wear flip flops, sandals, or any other open-toed shoes. A business suit or an outfit with a professional coat is preferred. Makeup is generally encouraged, but keep it business appropriate.

For men, a well pressed button up dress shirt, tie, dress slacks, and dress shoes are a minimum. A matching suit jacket is preferred. A clean shave is usually the best way to go.

For both men and women, often, the more traditional the attire, the better. If you feel you want to add a pop of color, texture, or other details that might make you more memorable, use accessories like a bright tie (for men) to compliment a suit, or wear a professional statement piece of jewelry (for women). Avoid showing tattoos. You shouldn't wear over-bearing colognes or perfumes. The key is to have a presence without being overwhelming.

Lastly, ensure that you have given your full attention to personal hygiene including modest deodorant, tooth brushing, flossing, and mouthwash. While it is not expected that every job applicant looks like a movie star or television news anchor, it is important to present a neat and clean appearance.

Good Manners

Another way to make a statement is by remembering your manners. Etiquette is no longer taught and often forgotten. Therefore, when used, it is noticed. If you want to stand out and be remembered, mind good manners. Here's a few tips:

1. Address. Always address someone new using "Mr." or "Ms." and their last name. Use "Mrs." with their last name only if you are sure they are married. Use "sir" or "ma'am," "yes, sir" or "yes, ma'am," unless directed by them not to. You can call them by their first name if they grant you permission. Ensure you give your full respect to their name even if the interviewer is younger than you.
2. Handshake. A handshake may not be the norm given the Covid 19 environment, but it has been a professional standard for ages, so if it is allowed, attempt it. Give a firm, short handshake. Don't squeeze too hard, and don't let your hand turn into a limp fish. If needed, practice handshakes with others who use them often and ask for their advice.
3. Cell phones. Keep your smart phone on silent so you can pay full attention to your interviewer. You can reference your phone, if needed, but never answer or view it when someone else is trying to call or text you. One example of an appropriate use would be to consult your calendar if your interviewer has a question about a particular date for a project you worked on.
4. Slang. Avoid slang. For example, say "yes" instead of "yeah" or "uh-huh." Say "no" instead of "nah-uh." Say "because" instead of "'cause."
5. Curse words. Avoid curse words and religious references of any kind. For example, say "darn" instead of "damn" when describing situations or telling stories. Say "oh my goodness" instead of "oh my God."
6. Say please. Always say "please," and "thank you!" If asked if you would like a water, it's "yes, please" or "no, thank you."
7. Thank you. Before exiting your interview, you should always thank the person for their time and let them know you are appreciative.

There are many other points of etiquette that often seem like common sense to some, but are somehow never considered by others. The more thoughtful and polite you are, the better the impression you will make.

Being polite and having good manners is important in remote interviews as well. Remember to be on time and be on your very best behavior for all interviews, regardless of the type.

What to Bring to an Interview

Knowing what to bring is an important part of being prepared and mentally ready. Here are some suggested items that should be gathered in advance, so you don't feel rushed when the interview time actually arrives:

1. Interview instructions. You should read any interview instructions as soon as you get them from the interviewer or the company to ensure you can be prepared. It could also be helpful to bring these instructions with you in case you need to quickly read it again before the interview.
2. Job application. If there is a job application, always try to get a form and prepare it in advance of the interview. If you were able to complete it online, bring a printed copy which might be helpful.
3. Resumé. Ensure you have additional copies of your resumé in the event the interviewer didn't bring it, forgot it, or perhaps wasn't even given it. Also be sure to offer it right away – letting the interviewer know you have a copy if they need it shows you are proactive and helpful. You also want to have a copy for yourself in the event you are asked about something specific. You can easily refer to it and clarify any items.
4. 90 day plan. If you prepared a 90 day plan, bring a few printed copies with you.
5. Consider bringing any additional paperwork that you can put in front of the interviewer to help make a compelling argument that you are the best candidate for the job and are fully prepared for day 1.
6. Letters of recommendation or references. If you don't have letters or documents available, having the contact information for your references

would be good. It is also helpful if you have already contacted these references and asked permission to list them so a call regarding you would not be a surprise. You can also simply keep a list of references handy and then provide it only if you are still interested in pursuing the position.

7. Pen and paper. Always bring a pen and paper to write down any notes, dates, or key information discussed during the interview. Ensure you write down the name or names of the interviewers. You will need this to send them a thank you note after the interview. Ask if they have a contact email they can provide should you have any additional questions. Don't spend the whole time trying to document everything in your notes. You should be focused on the conversation with the interviewer. However, writing a few things down indicates you are organized and professional, and can follow up on items without needing a reminder.

8. Identification. Bring your US passport, or two other items showing identification and eligibility to work (driver's license or identification card, social security card, or birth certificate).

9. List of questions for the interviewer. Bring some questions in advance. Have this list handy during the interview so you can quickly add to it if needed. At the end of the interview, ask if there is a little time available to ask a few questions.

10. Ensure you have some time after the interview to be available for a tour of the facility or perhaps onboarding paperwork, just in case!

11. Bring energy, positivity, and your smile!

7

Preparing for the Interview

To get the job, you need to put your best foot forward in the interview. We have already mentioned that the better prepared you are, the better your chances. It is a recurring theme! Of course, part of preparation includes the resumé you send before the interview. But you should also consider your method of delivery as well as your entire presentation. You are trying to sell yourself and therefore you should think of yourself as a highly valued product from application to interview. There are some tips and tricks you can use to set yourself apart.

Hiring managers use interviews to weed out some candidates as well as move others forward in the process. Therefore, preparation is paramount. You have hopefully already researched the company, read the latest annual report, and have an idea of company's mission, products and services. You need to research and prepare your answers as to how you fit into their organization.

90 Day Plan

If you have ever been in a similar role to the position you're interviewing for, develop a 90 day plan of what you hope to achieve. Just be cognizant that you don't want to come across as arrogant with nothing to learn. Being a disrupter from your first day generally isn't a good plan.

There are three main benefits to a having an action plan. First, it shows that you have considered your role and focused on how you will be productive from day one. Second, it shows that you are proactive and capable of self-management and are already taking steps that will help integrate you into the team quickly. Finally, you are showing you can set goals and align them to the needs of the organization.

Your 90 day plan should have your goals and action steps laid out and aligned with the company's mission and goals. Computer applications such as Microsoft's Powerpoint offer a good platform to organize and present your plan. Your goals should revolve around acclimating, performance, and your personal goals. Here are some Goal and Action examples:

1. Goal: Learn how job duties are completed in the position
   Action: Shadow employees with similar role and ask questions as needed
2. Goal: Expand knowledge of company's business
   Action: Study and learn about all of the company's products.
   Action: Schedule quick meetings with key team members and ask questions
3. Goal: Improve on job duties and time to completion
   Action: Learn company systems and processes and focus on consistent delivery

Setting your goals and taking time to consider the action steps that are needed can often be generalized as shown above. However, the more thought you put into how your goals and your actions can align to a company specifically, the more effective you will be. Take care in making sure that your goals and actions flow smoothly and make sense. Review your plan with your supervisor and make any adjustments as necessary based on their feedback.

Some additional examples of goals and action items could be:

1. Goal: Getting to know the team
   Action: Set reasonable timelines for completion

Action: Set up daily or weekly one on one meetings with coworkers
Action: Verify inclusion in invite lists and appropriate meetings
2. Goal: Performing job duties
Action: Meet with manager for necessary feedback
Action: Observe and ask questions as appropriate

Once hired, you can use these goals for your performance reviews, which is really just another interview for employees already on board.

Types of Interviews

It's worth noting that there are several types of interviews. We often believe that when we get an interview, we will sit on the opposite side of a desk or conference table from a person who will ask the questions. However other types of interviews exist and are used frequently. Consider the following interview types:

1. The one-on-one interview. This is the most widely used, most traditional option for an interview. These are often used by small and medium businesses due to their limited managerial staff. Candidates would interview with the owner or manager only and a decision is made. However, you could have a combination of first doing a one-one-one with a manager, recruiter or HR representative and then move to a second phase of interviews that could be individual, group or peer interviews. One-on-One interviews could be in person (face-to-face), by telephone, or by video call.

2. The group, panel or team interview. Often you may sit in front of a group or panel. Sometimes this might be your first interview, or it could be the last in a string of interviews. It will ultimately depend on the position and the company's process. In general, you will be notified if this is the case. Most often, you will sit in front of two or more people and each person will be tasked with asking you specific questions as it relates to their interactions with the position you will be considered

for. Sometimes the panel is all from the same department related to the position, and sometimes they are managers from different departments all looking to add the best all-around person for the company.

3. Peer interviews. Some larger companies will have you interview with your potential coworkers in the group you will be working in. Peer interviewers rarely make the hiring decision, but they can certainly influence the hiring manager on if you would be a good addition to the team. Peer reviews are often done when you are already an employee and going through a quarterly or annual review process, or when being considered for a promotion or transfer.

4. The job fair or screening interview. When at a job fair, you might be asked to fill out an application and answer a few screening questions to determine if you should be considered for a more formal interview. Recruiters and HR managers often do the screening. They will look at your resumé, have a brief conversation with you to screen whether you should be considered for the next phase of interviewing.

5. The testing interview. A testing interview usually involves testing your skills and competency in specific areas. Tests could cover critical thinking, spelling and grammar, math, keyboarding speed and accuracy, computer application or programming skills, or other job related skills. The tests depend on the skills expected and the job duties of the position. For example, you might have to take a physical test like showing you can lift fifty pounds if the job requires lifting.

6. One-way interviews. Usually an automated type of interview where questions have been pre-determined and the candidate sends in their responses. Some companies are now utilizing a system to ask you questions while capturing a video of your responses, that will be reviewed by the company at a later time, as they evaluate all of the submissions received by candidates.

7. The information or exploratory interviews. This type of interview is more often conducted with you being the interviewer. You schedule an interview with a recruiter, manager or employee of a company to gain insight and information about a company you are considering for

a position. You research the company and prepare questions to ask so that you can better understand if you would want to work in the field, industry or for that company.

Also, consider the following interview methods:

1. In-person interviews, on-site interviews. Traditionally, the most common type of interview was an in-person, on-site interview. You would typically meet face-to-face with the small business owner, department manager, or human resources manager in their office.
2. In-person interviews, off-site interviews. You may find that an owner of a small business or a recruiter will ask to meet at a coffee shop or other off-site location. This is due to a lack of privacy or meeting space at the business location, or sometimes to keep the fact that they are interviewing candidates confidential.
3. Virtual (remote) interviews. Virtual interviews, also known as Remote Interviews, can take place via phone or online video call. There are various video platforms and technologies that companies may use such as Google Duo, Microsoft Teams, Zoom, WebEx, etc. These types of interviews are becoming much more common in the new hybrid and fully remote working environments.

Knowing what type of interview, and what interview method you will participate in, helps you prepare for your best presentation. A one-on-one, in-person interview will feel very different than a remote (virtual) interview. A screening interview, is much different than a panel interview. However, if you feel confident in what you are looking for and why, have tailored your resumé and cover letter for the position, and have researched the company well, you will be better prepared for whatever may come. Believe it!

8

Remote (Virtual) Interviews

We now live in a new world where technology is available to do interviews remotely. However, a remote interview can take some extra planning and preparation. A remote interview can sometimes invade on your personal space. If you are doing a remote interview from home, there are a few things to keep in mind in addition to your appearance and manners. You want to make your first impression your best, so prepare your space, camera, and laptop at least a few days in advance, if possible.

Remote (Virtual) Interview Set Up Tasks:

1. Platform. Be sure you know which platform you will be using. Is it Zoom, Microsoft Teams, Google Duo, or some other platform? If you are trying to figure this out five minutes before your interview, and you haven't downloaded and set up the necessary application, you could end up being late or missing the interview altogether. If it is a platform you are not familiar with, be sure to watch a tutorial or YouTube video on how to use the platform in advance.
2. Device. Whether using a laptop, tablet, or smart phone, make sure it supports the video call platform and is ready and available for use. Check to ensure your device is able to connect to the internet if needed to support the call. Plug your device in! Never rely solely on battery

power for your device during the live interview. If possible, make sure you also have a fully-charged backup battery available.

3. View. Is there an appropriate wall, such as brick, that would appear modern or professional from the camera's point of view? Be aware of what the video call camera can view in the background behind you during the call. Remove any clutter and make sure the background is professional looking.

4. Virtual backgrounds. If you are struggling to find an appropriate, professional area, investigate some of the virtual backgrounds offered by the various video conferencing platforms. Avoid backgrounds that look obviously fake or distracting. Avoid vacation type backgrounds, such as a beach, since this is meant to be a professional interview.

5. Camera angle. The camera should be raised near eye level or slightly higher. You should be seen from at least the shoulders up and centered in the camera's view. If you don't have a desk available, consider using a tripod or extra chair to set the proper height for the device. If you need more height, consider a box or stack of books to get the best possible camera angle.

6. Lighting. Check your equipment's lighting to be sure it is working and that the results look professional. Adjust blinds and drapes as needed. Poor lighting can ruin an interview. Your session should make your video feed appear clear and well lit. A room that is bright with light may make you look more energetic and optimistic.

7. Sound. Ensure the sound quality is professional. Consider purchasing or borrowing an external microphone for better sound quality during your interview. Test it.

8. Quiet. You want to be sure you have a space that is quiet and devoid of any potential interruptions or distractions. Set other cell phones and devices to silent mode to avoid noise distractions. If preparing for a remote interview from your home office, if at all possible, try to ensure any other house members are completely out of the house at least an hour before the scheduled interview. If there are children in the home, can another family member schedule an activity out of the house for

them during this time? Ensure dogs that like to bark are also in another room or out of the house with other family. If others will be staying in the house, perhaps adding a "please do not disturb" sign on your room door indicating that an interview is in process. Everyone needs to know that you have an important interview at a prescribed time.

9. Pen & paper. Have a pen and paper handy to write down any notes, dates, or key information discussed during the interview. Not only will this help you keep track, it will also convey to the interviewer that you are serious about the position.

10. Resumé and 90 day plan. In addition to your resumé that you gave the interviewer, also have a copy printed and quickly available for your reference, if needed. Also have your 90 day plan printed and available if you prepared one for the position. Unless you are very comfortable with the platform, don't try to access your documents on the same device that is hosting the live interview. Instead, use a second device, or just use the information printed out. Alternately, you can request the email address of the interviewer and send them your resumé or 90 day plan so they follow along during the call.

11. Questions for the interviewer. Have questions prepared in advance that you can easily reference. Perhaps writing them on note cards so you don't have to adjust your computer setup is a safe way to go.

Practicing with your setup, on the same platform the interview will be using, is probably your safest way to ensure it will all work as expected. If possible, have a friend call you in advance using the same platform so you can be confident your setup works and will look professional from their view.

During the Interview Video Call

There are some key items to keep in mind during your interview video call. While they may seem minor, if you don't get these right, it can become annoying and may give the impression that you are unprepared or not proficient with today's technology.

1. Eye contact. Ensure you are looking into your camera and not your laptop or device screen. Your interviewer may think you are distracted and looking at something else.

2. Voice. Make sure you project your voice towards the microphone. It is also good to confirm if the interviewer can hear you well.

3. Body language. As with an in person interview, ensure you are sitting up with good posture and attentive to the camera just as if you were live in person.

There are some additional suggestions that are also applicable to phone interviews, so review those as well.

Phone Interviews

You might think of phone interviews as irrelevant. However, with the new Covid-19 business environment and various governmental mandates or company policies on in-person contact, phone interviews have come back more frequently. Additionally, many companies are doing phone interviews prior to setting up an in-person interview, especially if the job requires relocation.

Keep in mind that a phone interview can be more stressful than an in-person or video interview if only for the fact that we depend on body language when we communicate, and this will be absent on both sides. Nonverbal cues give additional context to what is being said. We normally depend on facial expressions, posture, eye contact, and hand gestures to bring clarity to a conversation. When these nonverbal cues are absent, the conversation becomes one dimensional. Thus, it becomes imperative to consciously adapt and compensate for the absence. Some tips to help make a phone interview go more smoothly are:

1. Manners. Don't forget your manners. Establish rapport in the beginning with proper introductions. For example, when they give you their name, title and company, you should acknowledge with something like, "Hello,

Mr. Patterson, it is a pleasure to have the opportunity to speak with you. I know you are a very busy person."

2. Excuse yourself. If you are busy or in a crowded place, ask the person to give you just a moment to move to a more quiet place.

3. Be engaged 100%. Find a place where you are not distracted and can focus your attention 100%. Turn other devices such as radios, televisions, etc. off.

4. Phone etiquette. Speak slowly and clearly. Don't speak over the interviewer. Wait until they have finished talking before responding.

5. Pause. We are naturally uncomfortable with silence. However, don't be afraid to take moments to pause and think about a response. You can always ask the interviewer for a few moments to consider a response. If an answer doesn't come, you can always ask if the interviewer can come back to a question to allow additional time to respond appropriately.

6. Don't use a cell phone speaker. A cell phone's speaker and microphone quality can sometimes be poor, letting in background noise or interference that can make it more difficult for the interviewer to hear you.

9

Sample Interview Questions

The secret to mastering an interview is to anticipate what will be asked and then have some well thought out responses. Often, questions will be common— easy and very generic. Even if they don't ask precisely these same common questions, many of these responses are universal enough that they can still end up being used as part of a great response to their question. However, there are times when a curve ball is thrown. Perhaps they ask a technical question and the answer is completely unknown to you. Perhaps the question itself seems bizarre or the reason they are asking a question makes absolutely no sense to you. The good news is that you can prepare and practice for all of these types of questions.

Common Questions

Some of the most common straight forward questions asked that you can practice responses to include:

1. "Tell me more about yourself"
   Use the time to make a positive impact that would support you being the best candidate for the job. Offer information that contributes to the story you are trying to convey. Do you have any positive hobbies like painting or playing an instrument? Any recent travels focusing on your

energy to explore new things, or recent goals and accomplishments? Do you have a previous job, experience, education, or inspiration that brings some flavor to get the conversation going about this new job opportunity you are considering? Share it! Volunteer or charity work can be good to add, but keep them brief. Keep in mind that the key to sharing your response to such an open ended question is to know when to finish your story, so you can move on to more job-related questions. When answering personal questions like this, be sure to keep it light and middle of the road. Keep in mind that you are being judged. Don't be an open book with all of the negative information. Always paint yourself as a neutral portrait. Keep religion and politics out of the conversation. Don't share recent death and divorce stories, injuries, etc. You are not trying to gain sympathy and it could end up being an awkward conversation. Most people don't know how to react or respond to bad news. The worst part about doing this is that it takes time away from positive information that you could be sharing instead.

2. "What experience do you have that you can bring to this role?"
Remember this doesn't have to be direct job experience. Think of how all your talents and experience can translate. Are you naturally an organized person? Can you bring organization to a system or process? Are you a good mentor through a charitable organization? Discuss how it can translate to what you can bring to the job role. Stay positive and energetic.

3. "Where do you see yourself in 3-5 years?"
An interviewer will ask this question to gain perspective on if you see upward mobility with the company or if the job is just a temporary stepping stone and you will move on the first chance you get. It is expensive to recruit, hire, and train new employees, so organizations often want to invest in people that plan to stick around. Be enthusiastic and show some ambition to learning and working the role before considering other things.

4. "What are 3 of your strengths and 3 of your weaknesses?"

   Your strengths probably already align with what you listed on your resumé. Highlight them! Saying one of your strengths is "teamwork" because you enjoy working hard and being part of a winning team is almost always a good response that aligns with most companies. Regardless of what you choose to say, don't just list out the 6 words. Expand on why you consider something to be a strength or weakness. For any weaknesses you share, be sure to include what you are doing to address the weakness. Don't just play a victim. Recognize a shortcoming, but share a positive outlook that indicates you are working to improve. As a side note, don't get too worried about what you choose. You may feel that being competitive is a strength, but the organizational culture might favor collaborative teamwork instead. What you may see as a weakness, the organization might find as a strength. For example, some may consider having a lack of experience as a weakness. Yet, many companies want to hire employees who don't have experience since they prefer to train you the way the want before you have had a chance to develop any preconceived notions about how things should be done. A lack of experience can also mean you have a fresh perspective, or you are more hungry or enthusiastic than someone that may be stuck in the status quo. The important thing is to show in the interview that you can spend some effort to reflect on yourself, and then select some words that align with who you are and what you can bring to the company.

5. "Describe a challenge you faced and how you solved it."

   This is your opportunity to showcase your problem solving skills. An opportunity to show how you overcame adversity. Answering this question doesn't always have to be related to a past job experience, but select stories showing your tenacity and handling of a difficult situation that can translate to the position. Select any stories that can highlight how you can think quickly, process information, get creative, organize, or bring people together during a crisis to do something positive for the team or organization. Stories of workplace struggles and achievements are preferred to address this question. Stories of personal struggles and achievements, such as dealing with a major health issue, recent divorce, home foreclosure, etc, should be avoided. You don't want to come across as a victim or someone who should be pitied. Instead, the focus should be on the achievements side. If the achievement you are describing can align well with a goal of the organization, you have just strengthened your case for being a great new hire.

6. "Why do you want to work here?"
   Remember that you want to show that your goals and ambitions are aligned with those of the company. Think back to the previous chapter on company research and consider the company's mission, culture, work-life balance, etc. Share something that aligns well. Is there room for advancement, or do you believe the work will challenge you? Understandably, we often choose to work somewhere because we need a job, and this company happens to be hiring. Don't say that, instead, be more creative in how you answer. You could say that the company originally caught your attention because you had decided to make a move and their opening seemed to be a good fit. Further, once you researched the company, you found other benefits the company offered such as positive work culture, training, or opportunity to learn in a new industry too much of an opportunity to pass up without finding out more.

7. "Why did you leave, or are you leaving, your last job?"
   If you are currently employed, this question is almost always asked. You want to be prepared to answer it, but avoid being negative. Don't criticize the company, the job, boss or coworkers. A safe and simple answer may be that you simply felt you have outgrown the position. If you didn't get the promotion, raise, or bonus you expected, don't say that. You can simply say that your advancement was limited by the current structuring of the business. Remember to be gracious. You can

explain that you have been appreciative of the opportunity the company gave you and there are no hard feelings. Pivot back to experience or skills you gained there and how you can apply them to the position you are interviewing for.

8. "What type of work do you enjoy the most?"
   This question is an opportunity for the interviewer to determine if your interests, strengths, personality, and traits, align with the position. If possible, integrate your strengths and traits to the job description, culture, and duties. For example, if the job requires work to be done through collaboration and teamwork, you could say that you enjoy collaborating with a team to obtain extraordinary results. You could say that you enjoy learning best practices from others which improves your own skills and capabilities and that you can easily adapt and adjust to how teammates work. However, if the job description is looking for someone with analytical abilities who can work on their own, you may want to emphasize your problem-solving skills. You could say that you can work independently when needed, take pride in your work, and quality matters to you. If possible, paint a picture of these skills in action by discussing a project you completed where you identified, analyzed, and solved an issue that resulted in a positive outcome. Regardless of what you say, it is good to be honest with yourself and the interviewer.

9. "Are you willing to work weekends, holidays, or overtime?"
   It is best to consider this question early on when exploring industries and companies. For example, retail, service and technology industries often work weekends, evenings, holidays and overtime. If the position doesn't usually expect you to cover these days and hours, you can respond by asking for more information such as "How often does that occur?" Their response can give you a window into what type of commitment they are expecting for this role. If it is infrequent, stay positive, and say you are always happy to add value when needed. However, if it is a regular occurrence and these types of hours won't

work for you, it is best to be honest and say so upfront.

10. "What motivates you?"

The interviewer could be trying to get a vision of whether your motivation aligns with the job and benefits offered. Or, they could be looking for an indication that money isn't so important in the event their offer in pay is lower than the industry standard. You could say something like "I love finding ways I can add value to whatever needs to be done," or "I really enjoy being on a team that has ambitious goals." Another response might include something like "I enjoy finding ways to make work more efficient," and then elaborate on the satisfaction you had when you completed a process improvement project and saw some amazing results. If you are motivated by compensation such as bonuses, commissions, or pay increases, don't be afraid to say so, but keep it lighthearted. Most employees working for a living are motivated by money and enjoy being recognized when they add value to a company. You can say that you're motivated when you are rewarded for your exceptional work contributions. Many companies have a multi-faceted approach to recognition that not only includes financial rewards, but other benefits such as employee recognition, awards, company branded merchandise, or time saving perks like premium parking. If the company has a wall for "employee of the month," and you find that encouraging, now is the time to say so. Just remember, whatever you respond with, show them your enthusiasm for the position and opportunity to do the work.

11. "What do you know about our company?"

You might be asked to explain what you know about the company, so be prepared. You did the research, so you should know what product or services they provide. You should have an idea of how many locations they have, how many employees, recent news, etc. Most importantly, it is good to share a quick sentence about their newest product or plan for growth so they know that you are fully committed with where they are going into the future. Be sure to memorize or have notes with you that highlight any key data points. Be sure to frame what you know in the positive.

12. "What would your current manager or coworkers say about you today?" Frame your response to be positive. If you are frequently late, you may want to avoid mentioning it. However, you could say that your manager might say you work well under pressure, or are committed to helping the company catch up when demand spikes. The answer probably isn't necessarily as important as just having an answer. You surely don't want to say, "I don't know." This could indicate that you lack self-awareness in how you fit in with your company or team. Perhaps respond back with one of your three strengths and briefly highlight any recent examples.

13. Questions related to being fired or laid off
Briefly provide a high level summary. Say what you learned from the experience and how you took some time to learn something new or gain more insight into your career options. Practice your response with others and go with the version that you can most comfortably relay in a brief manner. Don't go into detail unless asked. Keep it concise. Demonstrate in your response that you are focused on the future and excited to get started.

14. Questions related to gaps in employment
Inevitably, if you have spent any amount of time in the workforce, there is a good chance you have a gap in employment. Many times, there is a simple explanation. Perhaps you transitioned from college to the workforce or maybe the company you worked for went out of business unexpectedly. If your gap in employment was brief, you shouldn't have a concern over how you will respond when asked about it. Sometimes you can also craft your resumé so that gaps are minimized. For example, perhaps you can drop the months and just list the years of employment, such as "May 2016 – February 2019" simply becomes "2016 – 2019."

This works for gaps that are a year or less. Gaps longer than a year could certainly start a conversation. Your best defense is to be prepared for the question. Keep your response positive and honest.

If the gap is for personal reasons, such as you moved, relocated, had a baby, needed to care for a sick family member, or just took some time off, briefly explain how the time was needed and also what you learned during the experience. Did you grow personally as you overcame a challenge? Did you learn or read something new to help you navigate the experience? How can this experience translate to this new position, if hired?

If you have been job hunting the entire lapse in employment and haven't landed a job, take some time to really decide how you want to convey this. You don't want to say that you were laid off and have been looking for another job since, but haven't had a single interview. While that might be true, you should consider rephrasing. You could say that you had the opportunity to be more selective in your search to find a good fit. You could explain that the right opportunity just hasn't come up yet. Keep the conversation brief, but be sure you explain the time gap with any new experience you gained. Then, work to transition the conversation back to your relevant skills and experience. Convey that you believe you have the capability to start performing in the job on the first day of work.

Technical Questions

If you are applying for a position that requires some technical knowledge or skill, these can be a bit more challenging to anticipate. Start by re-reading the job listing details including the knowledge or skills required for the position. If you know someone that has been through a similar interview, ask them for some advice. Research, study, and practice. Even if you are proficient, it is always good to do some amount of refresh preparation.

Sometimes they may ask a technical question, similar to a math problem, and you either know it or you don't. If you know it, great, answer it! If not, don't try to fake it. But also, don't give up there. If you don't know an answer, simply do your best to estimate, and then mention that you're never afraid to ask for help if you don't know something. You can also mention that you are a resourceful person and would diligently use available resources to find the best solution. You can also say that for matters of significant importance, having another team member or supervisor double check your work is a good practice to ensure quality.

If, during the interview, it appears you don't have quite the knowledge or skills they are looking for in a position, it never hurts to ask if there are ways you can expand and improve by attending additional training, taking night classes, or being mentored by someone more senior. Your enthusiasm and attitude in these situations can sometimes make a big difference.

Bizarre Questions

Some interviewers in larger companies may want to put you on the spot with some bizarre question or scenario. There isn't always necessarily a right or wrong answer to these questions. For these types of questions, the interviewer is focused on how quickly you can think on your feet and also perhaps to see how you respond under stress.

If you get asked a very out-of-the-ordinary question, take a slight pause and then ask for clarification to the question. Don't panic. Stay calm. Think of what you want to say before you blurt out the first thing that comes to mind. You may not even get a bizarre question, but just in case you do, at least you may be just a little more prepared than the other candidates. There are several types of bizarre questions, but most fall into the following four categories.

1. Brain teasers.
   One very well used type of bizarre question is "How many _____

will fit in a _____." For example, the interviewer might ask, "How many balls will fit in a school bus?" You could respond by saying, "It depends." This is almost always a great answer because it gives you time to pause and then turn the tables on the interviewer. The interviewer will surely ask, "It depends on what?" Then, you can start in on a long list of variables that would impact an accurate answer. You can ask, "What type of balls, beach balls, bowling balls, or tennis balls? Is the bus an airport type shuttle bus or more of a standard 40 foot long school bus? Is the bus full of people, or is it otherwise empty? Does the bus have overhead compartments?" The more questions you can rapid fire off, the better. Also, don't be afraid to be a little bizarre in your questions back to the interviewer such as, "Can I deflate the balls before I load them on the bus?" You are now showing that you can switch your conversation from something expected to unexpected and begin analyzing. Once you get to the end of your line of questioning, and have been provided some answers to your questions, then lay out a formula for how you would figure out an answer. "Ok, if the bus is 40 feet long and I can fit approximately 40 soccer balls every foot of length, that would equal to about 1,600 balls to fill the bus." Just give a best guess. Again, the answer isn't the test, rather it was your reacting, thinking, analyzing, and estimating that they were focused on.

Another sample brain teaser question is "How much does a Boeing 747 jumbo jet weigh in pounds?" Again, they are looking to see if you can analyze and break down a problem. You could ask questions yourself like, "Is the jet carrying passengers and luggage? Is the jet full of fuel?" It doesn't really matter, but it shows you are looking at various case scenarios and considering all the information before making too many assumptions. Once you demonstrate your thoughtfulness of the question, you can form a process to solve the problem. You could respond by saying, "Of course, we could do an internet search and find an estimate pretty quickly. Or, I'm pretty sure the airplane manufacturer could provide us with an extremely accurate answer using the model specifications. However, I assume you want me to estimate here on my own." You could then lay out that a standard jet is roughly equal to, say, 150 standard cars. If a standard car is roughly 3,000 pounds, then a jumbo jet would be roughly 450,000 pounds. Again, the actual math and answer isn't as important as your ability to break down a problem into smaller, more manageable pieces, do some quick estimates, some math by hand, and then state your best guess.

2. This or that.

   This is another odd interview question used for its simplicity. With a "this or that" type question, you are forced to choose one over another. Sample questions could be, "Cat or dog? Pink or blue? Beach or mountains?" For example, you could say "I like the beach because seeing, hearing, or feeling gentle ocean waves coming in always gives me a sense of renewal." It is usually not your answer that is important, but rather how you can respond to a question that hasn't been practiced. How do you respond to pressure and stress? Do you have reasons for your choices?

3. Imagine if.

   This question is often formed in reference to a scenario. One sample question is, "Imagine you were stranded on a desert island, and could only have two items with you, what would they be and why?" Another question is, "If you had superpowers, what would yours be, and how would you use it?" You can't really be prepared for these questions other than the fact you might get one, and if you do, stay calm and stay positive. Try to select an answer that you can support with a reason.

4. Morality.

   The morality questions are a little heavier sometimes. You are being put on the spot and can feel a little more exposed as to your answer. Just remember to pause, stay calm, and qualify your answer, if needed. Some sample morality questions are, "If you found $10,000 in an unidentifiable bag beside the road, would you keep it or what would you do with it?"

For these, it can certainly be that you would seek council from someone else such as a trusted family member, perhaps someone in your church, or perhaps even asking your supervisor for advice before ultimately deciding. Just keep in mind that you want to provide some answer, but you also want to convey that in some situations, it is ok to seek out appropriate experts since you earnestly want to do the right thing. You can also say you shouldn't rush important decisions unless you have to.

Once you have finished answering all the interviewer's questions, and hopefully there is still time left in the interview, you should pull out a short list of your own questions to ask.

Asking Questions

Never, never, never go to an interview without some prepared questions of your own. Asking the interviewer questions shows you have done research and actually have interest in the position and joining the company. Not asking any questions is a missed opportunity. It indicates that while you may be engaged in the analysis of "Am I a good fit for the company?" you have failed to consider the second analysis, "Is the company a good fit for me?" After they are done, you should start by telling the interviewer that you have some questions about the position and hope that they have a few extra minutes to spare. Then, you can start with your short list of questions (assuming they weren't already addressed during the interview) such as:

1. "Do you have a pay range identified for the position?"
   If the interviewer hasn't shared this information already, it is certainly the time to ask to ensure it aligns with your compensation expectations.

2. "If hired, where would I be working?" or "Do you offer remote work options?"
   Maybe they have a plan to move the office location to the opposite side of town in six months which could add an hour to your daily

commute. Perhaps you could work from home full or part time on a hybrid schedule. It would certainly depend on the position and job duties, but work location is a pretty important detail you want to be sure about.

3. "What traits make someone successful in this role?"
Not only does this give you a window of what types of key traits they are looking for in candidates, it helps you assess if you believe it aligns with what you're looking for.

4. "Can you explain the hiring process?"
Higher level jobs require more review. You may interview with HR and then later, a manager in the division you'll be working. For higher levels, there may also be a panel of interviewers. Knowing the process can help you mentally prepare and also make sure you can accommodate the timeline that may be involved.

5. "How do you handle promotions or professional growth of your employees?"
If you are considering the position as a foot in the door to something bigger in the organization, you will want to know if and how you could potentially have another opportunity.

6. "Can you describe the work culture?"
This may help you get the interviewer's perspective versus what you may have already read about the company during your research.

7. "Does the job require travel, relocation, working overtime, or special working hours?"
If the interviewer didn't bring the subject up, you should. You want to understand the expectations and not assume it isn't a possibility just because they didn't bring it up.

8. "Will the job require any special training or additional certifications?"
For example, employees involved in the preparation, storage, or service of food may be required to obtain a food handler's card. Some professional positions may have ongoing learning requirements. Special training for particular positions can vary and it is best to understand the requirements up front.

9. "Are you replacing someone or is this a new position?"
If you are hired and essentially replacing someone, there is the possibility that some coworkers could be sour to your entry. The interviewer may also tell you if the person was promoted or left the company. This information could help you be a little more prepared when interacting with coworkers who worked with your predecessor. Also, if it is a new position, you may need to mentally prepare to work in an environment where you have to blaze your own trail and figure some things out on your own.

10. "How long has this role been unfilled?"
Knowing the turnover rate of a position or how long a role has been unfilled could be a red flag unless there has been a hiring freeze or some other reasonable explanation.

11. "Is there anyone who had this same role that I can speak to in order to get more information?"
If they openly give you someone to talk to, that is a good sign! If not, consider why. Asking this question may also demonstrate to the interviewer that you are really interested in the position, but are just trying to get all available information to make sure it is a good fit before making a commitment.

12. "When do you anticipate making a hiring decision?"
Perhaps they intend to make a decision today or tomorrow, but it is also possible that they are required to keep the job announcement open for a

certain period of time. It's good to know if you are going to have to wait weeks for the job posting to close. This question is also a good way to find out exactly who the hiring decision maker is. The interviewer might reveal that they are not the actual one to make the ultimate decision, they simply provide a recommendation that then is approved by another manager, the CEO, or possibly, the board of directors.

Avoid asking questions about things that could easily be found on the company's website, social media, or any published reports. Basically, don't waste their time. There are probably lots of questions you really would be interested in knowing, so try to prioritize the most important ones first in case you run out of time. Remember that if they allow candidates the opportunity to ask questions, ask as many good questions as you can fit in.

It is impossible to account for every question that could come up. Just remember that the better prepared you are, the better your chances of not only getting the job, but having the potential of negotiating better pay, benefits, or other terms.

10

Handling Difficult Situations

When interviewing, we are sometimes so eager to impress the interviewer and get the job that we may overlook situations or issues that could potentially be red flags. All businesses from small to large have encountered ethical and legal issues related to topics like health conditions, racism, sexism, ageism, etc. Some companies have done a better job than others in addressing these concerns for their workforce. Of course, blatant discrimination is not usually what you deal with in an interview because most interviewers have received at least some basic training on this issue. However, it still may come up in some form during an interview or during some part of the interview process.

First, let's discuss prohibited employment discrimination in the United States. According to the US Equal Employment Opportunity Commission (eeoc.gov), applicants, employees, and former employees are protected from employment discrimination based on race, color, religion, sex (including pregnancy, sexual orientation, or gender identity), national origin, age (40 and over), disability or genetic information (including family medical history). These categories are commonly referred to as protected classes. Not all employers are covered by the laws that the EEOC enforces, and not all employees are protected. Coverage can vary depending on the type of employer, the number of employees it has, and the type of discrimination.

In regard to interviewing, this basically means that employers should not ask any questions regarding your status in a protected class. For example, if you are interviewing for a bartending position, the interviewer cannot simply ask your age. However, they can ask if you are over the age of 21, since you would need to be over 21 to dispense alcohol. Seek professional legal advice on these matters as it pertains to your particular situation.

Unfortunately, illegal discrimination in interviews still exists. If confronted, how should you respond? First, you should consider if the question offends you. It could be that this interviewer simply didn't realize that what they were asking could be offensive to you. If you feel it could just be an unconscious error, you could attempt to gently address it in a professional manner and try to move on. However, you may feel this question and resulting conversation is a red flag. Based on that, you could decline to answer the question, decide that this company is not a good fit for you, and move on to other job opportunities. Discrimination areas to be particularly aware of:

1. Racism

   You might be surprised, but yes, racism still exists in interviews. The practice could be very subtle by way of racism bias. Often, terms used in job postings or interviews may be used without the interviewer even recognizing the issue. Although many companies are making diligent efforts, even the biggest and best can still improve in this area. Employers need to always be considering the impact of their words as they continue to strive for the elimination of racial bias.

2. Ageism

   Discrimination based on age still exists and certain industries, such as information technology (IT), are well known for ageist practices. While "fresher" college graduates might have more skills related to current technology, interviewers shouldn't make the assumption that older candidates won't have current skills. While a college degree may be required for the position, asking "When did you graduate from college?" could provide an interviewer an easy way to estimate your age. Instead, they should simply ask if you graduated.

3. Sexism

   As with ageism, sexism is still an issue in the workplace. While interviewers are often aware of questions that are discriminatory, they sometimes may still ask. Here are a few examples that a female candidate may encounter:

   a. "Are you planning to have children soon?"

   b. "Have you considered applying for the secretary position?"

   It is important to note that sexism isn't only limited to female candidates, it can also happen to male candidates as well. The other protected classes may come up also.

How you can positively react to discrimination or offensive questions is what we want to focus on. First, try not to get defensive. This may sound counter-intuitive, especially if the question is highly offensive. However, keep your composure in the moment. Many times you may be encountering the interviewer's unconscious bias. The interviewer may not be aware of their misstep and simply need better training or guidance. Good companies may welcome feedback from candidates so that they can address issues going forward. However, it's usually not helpful to focus on that in the moment.

The preferred reaction is to pivot the conversation back to your relevant experience and skillset. Explain how you believe that question is irrelevant based on your success with a prior project or experience. If you did your research and truly believe this is a good company and one you want to work for, consider appropriately and politely addressing the discrimination after the interview or once you are hired. On the other hand, if during your research, you found other red flags, you might consider just completing the interview and then moving on to pursue opportunities with other companies.

Discrimination related issues may not be the only difficult situations you have to deal with during your job hunt and interviewing process. Topics around health can also be problematic. It can be difficult to know if, how, and when it is best to communicate these issues, and answers are not always straightforward. However, it certainly is good to give considerable thought to the approach you want to take regarding these topics.

Pregnancy

Should you or shouldn't you disclose if you are pregnant during an interview? There are very strong opinions on both sides. However, how you approach the topic could really depend on several factors.

First, when you researched the company, did you find they encouraged work-life balance? Do you find anything to support the idea that they are "family friendly?" When you walked into the office for the interview, did employees have pictures of their families on their desks? Further, is the position you are considering one that would allow for a leave of absence or the ability to work from home? If you answer all of these questions in the positive, then disclosing your news may not be as consequential as you originally thought.

However, you might want to keep your timing in mind. If you go into an interview and your physical condition is obvious, it is probably best to address it. An interviewer may avoid asking due to fear of discrimination, but they also may avoid considering you for the position. If you bring it up, then you at least have the opportunity to explain how you will handle the job duties, pregnancy, and the arrival of your baby. Give reassurance that you have carefully considered the impact to the company and are confident you can do the job.

You should also consider your timing as it relates to changing jobs while pregnant. If you have the luxury of choosing when you change jobs, you might want to consider changing jobs earlier in your pregnancy rather than later. If you make a move in your second trimester, you have the opportunity to get familiar with the job, acclimate to the culture and get to know your coworkers before taking leave. This could make working from home easier if given the opportunity.

Yet, if you wait to change jobs in your third trimester, you risk not being able to get up to speed in a new position. This could lead to stress and frustration for everyone. Further, if you unexpectedly go into labor early or have complications, you surely could end up in a situation where you and your new employer are scrambling to cover your work.

Illness or Other Health Conditions

Should you disclose a chronic illness or health condition? The short answer is that interviewers are not allowed to ask personal questions about your health or any disabilities. However, they can ask if you are able to perform specific tasks. For example, "Can you lift fifty pounds?" Now, does that mean you shouldn't disclose? The answer is, it depends. Like with pregnancy, if you are showing physical symptoms, it could be better to address it up front with confidence.

However, if you have a condition or illness that is not obvious, you have many other considerations to think about. First, will your illness or condition hinder your ability to do your job? Will your illness or condition require you to take more time off than normal? Will your condition worsen with time? Could your condition require emergency intervention by someone else while you're on the job? Unfortunately, not every condition or illness is predictable. Telling an employer that you are diabetic likely wouldn't hinder your chances of getting the job. However, it would be helpful to you and your coworkers that in the event your blood sugar triggers a seizure, they need to recognize your situation and intervene, if possible. In this instance, disclosure is likely beneficial. Now, on the other hand, should you disclose a condition that is easily managed by medication? Normally not, if it likely will never impact you performing your job duties.

Another consideration would be the company's benefits package. You probably shouldn't go into an interview and immediately ask if the health insurance will cover your illness or condition. Your best course of action if concerned about coverage would be to wait until an offer is made and you have a chance to discuss compensation and benefits in more detail. You could then bring up your condition to a representative that works in benefits, explain that you feel it is a non-issue and doesn't impact your ability to do the job. However, you would like to explore the health benefits and coverage.

Ask if they can call or provide you with a resource to confirm coverage.

Hopefully, you now have a starting foundation on how to consider your responses to interview questions based on your particular situation.

11

Things to Avoid in an Interview

Much of what you do and say in an interview should be considered carefully. We often focus on what we should do, sometimes it's good to be reminded of things you definitely shouldn't do. While some of these items are essentially the opposite of the things you should do, it's also included here because it is important and worth repeating.

Disrespect

Don't be disrespectful of people's time or their position within the organization.

1. Don't be late to the interview.
2. Sometimes the person you encounter in the parking lot, sharing the elevator, or tidying up the lobby area could actually be the owner, president of the company, or they could be your interviewer! Therefore, always be on your best professional behavior. Treat everyone with respect!
3. Don't allow yourself to be distracted. Silence your cell phone before you even walk into the office. You want to convey that this interview is the one and only thing on your mind and has your full attention.
4. Don't be distracting to others in the office. From the moment you

enter the office or interview to the moment you leave, don't distract those around you with being overly vocal or loud. Definitely don't say anything derogatory. Keep these thoughts in your head.

Body Language

You don't want to present yourself as being overbearing, impatient, or the worst, lazy. Follow these suggestions:

1. Don't slouch in your chair. Show great posture. Sit up! Don't rest your feet on something. This is not your living room at home. You should give the impression you are attentive, serious, and professional. Slouching can come across as being lazy.
2. Don't fidget. Being uncomfortable is understandable. However, if you fidget and can't seem to sit still, it can become very distracting to the interviewer. Don't chew gum. Don't incessantly click your pen. Don't constantly tap your feet on the floor or your fingernails on the table.
3. Don't give a limp handshake. If the interview is in-person, and Covid protocols allow, give a good handshake. Fist bumps are more practiced now, but also be ready to perhaps have no physical contact at all. If you do decide to go for a handshake, make sure it is firm, but not overbearing. Don't present your hand like a limp spaghetti noodle. Give a good shake, then release- don't linger like you're waiting for a handshake photo.

During the Interview Conversation

While you're speaking, try to treat the interview like a conversation that effortlessly goes back and forth. This will help reduce stress on your nerves and help keep your responses concise.

1. Don't talk too much. Yes, you need time to sell yourself and your capabilities, but if you have answered their question or provided a good example of your experience, just focus on finding a good way to wrap

up your response. You don't want to hijack the interviewer's process by talking too much about something that could be answered more efficiently.

2. Don't play the role of a victim. Don't make the interviewer try to feel bad for you by talking about your hardships, problems in your personal life, or why you are desperate for the job. As a matter of fact, never say or convey that you are desperate! Focus on positives and how you are moving forward.

3. Don't exaggerate everything. Being too over-the-top, outlandish, or animated with your stories and responses can become distracting and may turn the interviewer off. You can have a few moments to show you are a real person, but make sure they see that you can operate with a serious, professional side also.

4. Avoid getting too personal. Don't ask or comment about the interviewer's appearance or any obvious condition or disability. Unless asked, avoid sharing personal information that is not relevant to the interview or job.

5. Don't be overly ambitious. Don't express your ability or desire to take over as the company's president. Being ambitious and eager for promotion and growth is good, but convey that you're willing to put in the time and effort to become the best in this current job first. Interviewers may avoid candidates they believe will have dissatisfaction with their current job, or unrealistic expectations for a speedy promotion or career advancement.

6. Don't appear to be uninformed. Don't ask what the company's mission is or what product or service they provide. You should already have this information from your research. You can always ask for clarification, but don't show the interviewer that you didn't invest any time in trying to figure out the basics beforehand.

7. Don't interrupt. Never interrupt an interviewer's question or statement assuming you know what they are going to say. Doing this frequently can easily come across as disrespectful, arrogant, or brash. Refrain from speaking over them to make a point. Be polite and wait.

Assumptions

Trying to get a good understanding of a company, a department, or a specific job and how it fits in can often lead to making assumptions. However, there are certainly things you shouldn't assume:

1. Don't assume the interviewer has read your resumé. Many times it was a different person that reviewed it, which is what helped you get the interview. After all, getting an interview is the primary goal of a resumé. The actual interviewer may not have even seen a copy of your resumé yet, or if they did, perhaps they only had a few minutes to skim over it minutes before the interview. Therefore, don't assume they know how your listed skills or experience may best translate to the position. Regardless, never make the mistake of disrespecting an interviewer by saying, "It's on my resumé" instead of directly answering their question. You may have just lost your chance. Answer their question, then politely refer them to where it is listed on your resumé.

2. Don't assume you will ace the interview and therefore skip doing any research or preparation. If you avoid preparing or practicing some of your answers to common questions, you may end up failing the interview and losing out on a great job.

3. Avoid assumptions and making inappropriate comments regarding the federally protected classes the interviewer may personally belong to— race, color, religion, sex (including pregnancy, sexual orientation, or gender identity), national origin, age, disability or genetic information. For example, don't assume someone does or does not have a spouse or children when responding to a question they have asked. Don't respond with something that may highlight or reveal their age. As part of one of your answers, don't bring up your religion or ask theirs.

4. Avoid political assumptions. Don't assume people are in alignment with your political views. Don't bring up your political affiliations or assume or ask theirs. Political comments can lead to discussions stirring up strong feelings that may ultimately end up derailing your interview.

5. Avoid assumptions based on someone's name. Don't assume, based on their name, that people are male or female, part of a particular ethnic group, or from a certain country. Don't assume names are related. Just because the interviewer's last name matches the company's name or an owner, doesn't mean they are related. Yes, it's possible, but don't assume it or bring it up. Try to focus on the position and you as a great candidate for it.

Timing

Timing can be everything. If you try to predict an outcome too early, you could ruin your chances for opportunities you didn't expect.

1. Don't try to predict the outcome. Perhaps you think you are surely getting the job. You may think you are the top candidate, and so you coast along only to find out that you were passed over. Conversely, perhaps you think you've already lost it. You think you bombed the interview only to find out that they indeed made you an offer! Or perhaps they offered the position to a better candidate, but they still really want you also, so they are now internally considering you for another position not yet advertised. Don't give up before the finish line. Just relax and let the process play out. Staying positive and seeing the full process through is usually your best bet.

2. Avoid asking about benefits too early. Questions about paid time off, vacation days, holidays, etc. too early could give the impression that you are already thinking about taking time off or needing something immediately after being hired. Wait until after the actual job offer is made to you.

3. Ensure you understand the anticipated timing for their interview process. If you are interviewing for multiple positions or with multiple companies, it will be important to keep it all in mind to ensure you can make the best decision for your next job.

Common sense plays a big part in knowing what you should avoid in an interview. Sometimes, understandably, we get nervous, our brain fogs over, and we fumble. However, the more you prepare and practice for your interviews, the less nervous you will be. Practice will hep you navigate your way through an interview with confidence. Balance that with a little humility, and the better you will do!

12

Negotiating the Salary

Understandably, salary is the main consideration for most people when looking at changing jobs or careers. Knowing what your skills are worth and how to negotiate your desired salary is essential. However, one must keep in mind that while your base salary is the most important element of your compensation, there are other important benefits that could make a job with a lower salary more attractive overall. While some companies might offer a higher salary, others may offer additional compensation in the form of bonuses, commissions, stock options, tuition reimbursement, or paid time off. There may also be other important considerations such as better healthcare benefits, better work schedules, or hybrid or remote working options which can save on commute time. Understanding all of these components is important to enable you to make the best overall decision for you.

Things to consider when negotiating a compensation package are:

1. Base salary or hourly wage.
   Base salary or hourly wage is the consistent foundation for your regular pay. Be sure you know the amount you are willing to accept no matter what other benefits are offered. After all, this is the primary opportunity to negotiate the highest and best pay. Many other benefits are tied to

or calculated from this key figure. Once hired, pay increases could be limited, making increases to this number more difficult. Your best opportunity to get your desired pay is upon hire. Keep in mind that whatever you accept in a position will likely be your threshold into the future. For example, suppose you agree to $75,000 annually, but someone else negotiates $85,000 for a similar position. If you both receive annual raises of 3%, their income will continue to grow larger than yours. The initial discrepancy of only $10,000 grows larger by 3% each year that you both get the same 3% raise. When presented with an offer with a base salary, always pause, then ask if there is any flexibility to increase it. Asking this one question, can sometimes get you thousands of dollars more.

2. Performance bonus or commission.
   Sales positions aren't always the only jobs that can typically receive bonuses or commissions. Some companies may offer individual or team bonuses or commissions if certain numbers, called metrics, achieve desired targets. These metrics can be tied to financial elements such as sales volume, revenue growth or profitability. They can also be based on a myriad of tracked indicators such as production output, utilization, employee productivity, customer wait time, customer survey responses, etc. For some sales positions, commissions earned can sometimes be more than the base pay portion of their pay. Understanding how achievable the sales target is will be the key to understanding how much total pay can be earned.

3. Signing bonus.
   Some industries and companies will offer a signing bonus. After you have negotiated the highest base pay possible, ask if they would consider if a signing bonus could be added. Keep in mind that a signing bonus is a one-time payment. Signing bonuses usually will also need to be paid back if you don't stay for a prescribed period, such as 1 full year of employment.

4. Performance review.

   Companies generally have a regular time period where they review employee performance and pay. For sales positions, this is also the time they would set the sales target for the next period. It is good to know when that typically is so you have an opportunity to justify more pay based on your contributions to the company. While some companies may review compensation quarterly (every 3 months) or semi-annually (every 6 months), most will do it annually (once a year). The more frequently they review, the better your chances are to shine and ask for a raise or bonus.

5. Cost of living increases.

   Some companies don't implement cost of living increases. If they do, increases are generally small and adjusted annually. All employees may get the same percentage increase, such as 2% of their base salary. Many companies that provide a general salary increase or bonus to employees have included a cost of living increase as part of the justification for the general increase or bonus.

6. Stock option or discounted stock purchase.

   Many large corporations will offer stock options or discounted stock as part of an overall compensation package. Keep in mind that although stock can lose value, if the company is successful, they can become extremely lucrative. You need to evaluate your risk tolerance and know that timing your purchase or sale of the stocks is important. If you are unfamiliar with the stock market and making those types of financial decisions, you might want to consult a financial advisor about the risks and benefits.

7. 401(k) matching, profit sharing, and pensions.

   Medium and large businesses as well as government jobs usually have some type of 401(k), profit sharing or pension program. However, not all plans are created equal. You will want to study the offered plan in detail, ask questions, and understand the ways the plan can be beneficial to your situation. Most plans have a long list of rules and restrictions that must be followed. Some plans, like most under a 401(k), are tied to investments in the stock market which can either lose value or be very lucrative. While pension plans have almost completely phased out, some can still be found in state and local government positions.

8. Health and dental insurance.
   The need for healthcare benefits is a major priority for many employees. The cost of healthcare can literally bankrupt you if you have a health emergency without insurance. Not all insurance plans are the same. Some companies go all out and provide the best healthcare packages available, while others only provide a certain minimum level of coverage. Benefit plans normally have a portion that is paid by the employer and a portion that is deducted from the employee's pay for each pay period. Most companies will have various options with minimum plans that are more affordable, and more expensive plans that have better coverage. Reviewing the plans and determining the relevant health coverage needs for you and your family can be a large consideration in the overall job evaluation decision.

9. Vacation, holidays, and personal days.
   Everyone needs down time or time off to recharge. Some companies are better than others at recognizing this. Time off can be an extremely attractive benefit, especially if you are still getting paid during the time off. The number of hours of paid vacation, holidays, or personal days can literally be a deciding factor between two relatively similar positions. If one position gives you only 2 weeks of paid time off a year, while another provides 4 weeks of paid time off, that extra two weeks is essentially a 4% bonus. Some companies will allow you to start accruing time off immediately, while others may make you wait until you've been employed for 90 days or longer.

10. Relocation allowance.

    Some large national and international companies will pay to relocate you. Some companies will even offer assistance with selling your home, moving, and the purchase of a new home closer to where you'll be working. If you ever wanted to move to a new area or would ever consider moving to another corporate division based in another area, this could be a huge financial incentive since moving can be expensive! Recently, relocation allowances have been drastically reduced due to the increase in remote work options and working from home technologies.

11. Training programs and learning opportunities.

    Many organizations believe that it is better to promote from within than hire outsiders. Therefore, many offer strong training and education programs to help retain their best employees. Some organizations will even reimburse employees for the cost of tuition at an accredited college or university! Even if you already have a degree, you might consider an advanced degree or perhaps a training program specializing in an area conducive to your career growth.

12. Growth, promotion or advancement.

    Always consider lateral or upward mobility opportunities when deciding what company to work for. For example, perhaps you were hired in California, but the company has a division in Virginia closer to home and family that you may decide to pursue in a few years. Perhaps they cross train from one division or area to another, so there are frequently new opportunities to move into other areas as your expertise grows and interests change. Perhaps you are hiring in as middle management and the company normally promotes from within when higher level leadership leave or retire. Perhaps the position could be a great promotional stepping stone. Take these potentials into consideration when evaluating a prospective job.

You can now see that while salary is important, it certainly isn't the only thing to consider. The key is to keep an open mind and evaluate as many facets of the job as you can. If you are interviewing at a company that you really like and want to work for, the chances are that you may have other benefits beyond a paycheck that are valuable to you.

Don't be discouraged by the job hunting process, it is quite a bit of work! Just remember when sending resumés and cover letters out, it is important to not get emotionally attached to one job opportunity while dropping other leads. Your chances of getting a great job are increased if you can manage to cultivate two or more job opportunities at the same time.

13

Seeking Simultaneous Job Offers

While it may sound like energy wasted, one of the best ways to attract great opportunities and the highest pay for your skills is to seek multiple job interviews at different companies while generating offers at the same time. Having multiple interviews will increase your chances of success for multiple job offers. This improves your chances of not only landing the job you really want, but more bargaining power when negotiating for higher pay and benefits due to your perceived status as a top talent that is in demand.

It is human nature to want what we don't have. Much of the success at auctions is the bidder's desire to be a winner for something that others really want. If you have the skills and experience, and you set the stage properly, you can have a stronger negotiating position with multiple parties interested in you. Multiple offers coming in gives you the bargaining strength to drive the pay up and also the freedom to choose the best offer among many. It can prevent you from having to accept a lower than competitive offer.

While interviewing, plainly explain that you have other interviews and offers that may take a little extra time, such as a week or two, to explore and wrap up. Doing this could lead to better offers or even a higher "right now" offer that may be too good to pass up. Of course, don't act too overconfident. Stay humble and merely say you are doing your due diligence since you really want your next position to be a good fit. It is always good to be up front and honest. If you don't have other offers, don't lie by saying you do.

Once you have one interview scheduled, the clock is ticking to find your second. Keep focused with the preparation you have already done and know that getting a few more interviews with other companies and positions could benefit you greatly. Remember that you have aligned yourself to apply for jobs that fit your goals. Don't randomly throw darts hoping to hit the target because you simply need another job offer so you can say you have one. Use the preparation you have done to focus your search and attempt another job you would seriously consider.

You should start to see everything is now coming together. Not just your cover letter and resumé, but more importantly, how you can professionally present yourself by being humble while demonstrating confidence. Showing a presence without being obnoxious. Presenting good manners while being courteous, interesting, and social. Good networking and presentation should pay off by building multiple introductions and opportunities for interviews leading to multiple companies giving you offers.

Tips to Encourage Multiple offers

Chances are that if you have been on multiple interviews, you could be on your way to multiple offers. Keep these tips in mind:

1. Complete all interviews. Be sure to complete all interviews you have scheduled. You can't get multiple job offers if you cut yourself short and cancel additional interviews with other companies that might turn out better than you think.
2. Be honest and upfront. If an interview went well and you have other interviews lined up, let the interviewer know. Being honest and upfront goes a long way. If you think or know you have an offer on the way, politely let the others know.
3. Be timely. If they make an offer, ask how much time they can give you for a response. If you know offers are on the way or you already have one in hand, let the interviewer know your anticipated timeline. Ask them to consider extending the response date of their offer, say an additional

week or so if you need, so you can fully consider their offer and make the best decision for you and your family.

4. Ask for the offer in writing. There is nothing worse than hearing you will be extended an offer and then it never comes. Be sure you ask if there is intent on sending you an offer and if you can get it in writing. An offer in writing is a sign of commitment. If you have it in writing, you have a better chance at negotiating other offers. It is also good to get it in writing so all of the details can be spelled out in case you missed something in a verbal offer. Basic details commonly include position and title, base salary, opportunities for performance bonus, number of days of paid vacation time, 401(k) plans offered, health benefits offered, and anticipated start date.

5. Be respectful. If you are extended an offer and aren't ready to take it, ask for time to consider and talk it over with family. While they may be your backup plan, don't treat them that way. Only keep an offer open if you would truly consider taking it.

6. Accept as soon as you feel it's right for you. If you believe that the offer you have is a great one and based on your goals, know this is the best fit position with a competitive salary, don't wait until the last minute to accept the offer, accept it quickly! Offers can be rescinded at any time, and it could be devastating to you if you have waited unnecessarily, and then had the offer taken back before you accepted.

Comparing Multiple Offers

Once you have multiple offers, it is important to evaluate fully and quickly. How do you make a decision on which to choose? First, you should lay out the offers so you can compare each important component. List items such as salary, bonus, commission, retirement plan option (401(k), pension, etc), number of paid days off (holiday, vacation, etc), healthcare benefits, etc. Then list the job duties, culture, long term prospects for advancement, etc. Add any additional criteria that you feel is important for you to consider. Finally, define the overall pros and cons of each job.

Creating a simple table of this information will help you lay out and compare the major items while also ensuring you haven't overlooked something:

MULTIPLE OFFER COMPARISON

ITEM	JOB #1	JOB #2	JOB #3
Salary			
Bonus			
Commission			
Retirement Plan (401k, pension)			
Paid Time Off (in days)			
Healthcare Benefits			
Job Duties			
Culture, Environment			
Advancement Opportunities			
Overall Pros			
Overall Cons			

Once you have laid out the details, consider if you can leverage your offers against each other. For example, if the pay is more attractive at one company, but the paid time off is better at another, you can go back to each and ask if that particular component is negotiable. Approach each employer with the idea that you like their company and you feel your skills and goals match their culture but had hoped for a higher salary, or a bonus, or more paid time off, etc. Make each feel like they could be your top choice if only for the one item at hand. It is important to be honest. Show enthusiasm for each job offer and communicate in a timely and positive manner with all. If you don't communicate timely, you could find that your offer has been rescinded (taken back and no longer open). Once you have determined which offer you truly want to accept, accept it quickly, and then after they confirm your acceptance, communicate openly and honestly with the companies you didn't choose.

With this honest and open approach to negotiating, you can obtain a more competitive offer, and still retain integrity that you have acted professionally. Remember, things can always change, and there may be a time in the future you may want to pursue another position with one of the companies you didn't select. Your career goal should be to always try to expand your professional network in a positive way, not burn a bridge you later wish you hadn't.

14

After the Interview

Immediately after any interview you participate in, take the time to send thank you notes to each of the individuals you interviewed with. Send a thank you note regardless of whether you choose to pursue the position further or not. It is always a good idea to stand out from all the other candidates. You never know what can happen. Perhaps a new position opens up and they want to consider you for that. Perhaps one day, you might be back at this company looking for another job and you could be remembered positively by this one simple gesture.

Here is a sample thank you note you can consider sending:

Dear Mr. Patterson

Thank you for taking the time to consider me for the Supply Chain Manager position at Big Corporation. I enjoyed the opportunity to meet and learn more about the position and the exciting future of your company. I look forward to hearing from you soon.

Sincerely,
Ashley L. Holiday
(555) 555-5555

If the interview didn't go so well, or you do not believe it is the right fit for you at this time, you should still send a thank you note. For this situation, you could consider something like this:

Dear Mr. Patterson

Thank you for taking the time to consider me for the Supply Chain Manager position at Big Corporation. I enjoyed the opportunity to meet and learn more about the position and the exciting future of your company. Unfortunately, I do not believe the position is a good fit for me at this time. Even though our timing or goals for the position don't currently align, I would certainly like to stay in contact with you and your company to consider other potential positions that may be available in the future.

Sincerely,

Ashley L. Holiday
(555) 555-5555

If you have decided to no longer pursue an opportunity that you have interviewed for, in addition to the thank you note, it may be wise to contact the hiring manager or interviewer by phone to communicate your decision verbally. You never know if they already have a different position in mind that would be a better fit. Use this as an opportunity to develop a lead to the job you are really looking for.

III

WORKING THE JOB

15

Working Hard and Staying Humble

Now that you have the job you want, the process of setting goals and building your resumé may seem like a distant memory. You did your research, networked with others, hit the streets, made lots of calls, endured a variety of interviews, sold your skills, negotiated your pay and benefits, and finally accepted a new job which now brings excitement, anticipation, and perhaps a little anxiety. Let's get started!

Working Hard and Staying Humble

What does working hard really mean? Does working hard mean that your work must be excessively physical and mentally demanding? Does it mean you are always the first to come in the office and the last to leave? Does it mean you forgo all breaks, lunch periods, and vacation days? Does it mean that you must always give more than everyone else? Does it mean that you are saying yes to whatever is asked of you? While sometimes these things will occur when working hard, the answers to all of these questions is no.

Working hard means learning all you can to be efficient and effective in your role to produce a product or service that you and your company can be proud of.

Working hard is about:

1. Commitment. Be committed and diligent to see tasks through to completion. Strive to get results by doing all you can to reach your goals.
2. Quality. Make the necessary sacrifices to ensure quality. Although sometimes necessary, working hard doesn't always require us to deplete all of our physical energy. It is not just brute force. It includes the need to work smarter or more efficiently to maintain a quality process while having high standards.
3. Engagement. Be engaged in your work by being enthusiastic, prepared, and collaborative. Take time to understand the expectations and tasks while aligning your skills and experience to accomplish tasks with competence. Working hard might mean that you recognize when expectations and time frames are misaligned and offer solutions rather than complaints.

Humility is a soft skill that is widely recognized and highly valued. Being humble doesn't require you to be a doormat for others to walk on, although sometimes it can feel that way.

Being humble is:

1. Listening. Take the time to listen and learn from others. Everyone has something to teach. Even those with major character flaws can serve as a bad example to help you avoid their mistakes. Many of the most intelligent people spend more time listening than speaking.
2. Having empathy. Put yourself in other people's shoes. Try gaining an understanding for someone else's position. You never know what someone else has been through or is currently going through.
3. Asking for help and feedback. There is no shame in asking for help when you need it. Many people have a natural instinct to want to help others. Sometimes you may have to swallow your pride, but you may

also gain some respect. When you ask for feedback, it shows you value the opinion of others.

4. Being grateful. Accept the present and appreciate the good things. Remember your beginnings and where you came from. You didn't always have the knowledge, skills, experience, or professional relationships that you have now.

5. Reflecting. You cannot improve if you cannot reflect. Reflection enables us to celebrate what we did well and learn from areas where we could have done better.

Continue to Network

Once we start a new job, we often put our heads down and go to work. We get drawn into the organization and before we know it, we have lost contact with a vital part of our individuality. Networking, while seen as a self-promoting activity, can be so much more. As mentioned, being connected and being a connector can foster new opportunities whether looking for a job, or finding ways to work smarter in the one you have. However, there are many benefits to continue to network even after landing a new job:

1. Growth. Continue to network so that those bonds and partnerships can strengthen and grow. One day you may come to need your network again and if you have been keeping it alive, it will be there for you.

2. Access. By staying in contact with your network while adding additional key contacts, your network can grow and continue to provide you access to people, knowledge, and job opportunities.

3. Confidence. Networking can build your confidence by tuning your social skills and communication. Building confidence will give you the courage to tackle new challenges, improve your skills, and reach new heights.

4. Reputation. As you network and build your skills, your reputation grows. You can become known as a "go-to" person or even the MVP (Most Valuable Player). Your reputation will become more well-known,

giving you social currency that can make advancement easier.

In a new job, you will start networking with coworkers, managers and perhaps even customers or clients. These connections should not be in place of your past network, but rather should be in addition to your past network. Continue to build and maintain your network and you will find that it will serve you well.

16

Emotional Intelligence (EQ) and Fitting In

Emotional intelligence (called EI or EQ for emotional quotient), simply put is our capability to understand and manage our emotions when interacting with others. EQ includes the ability to empathize with others to diffuse disputes and resolve conflict in a way that is meaningful to everyone involved. Having a high EQ means you are highly self and socially aware. Often you are seen as having a good sense of intuition about situations involving people and are good at resolving conflict.

If you believe you aren't good at soft skills or don't have a high EQ, no worries! You can increase your EQ through practice. Self-awareness is a good place to start. Become aware of how you react to emotions and interact with others. If you say things such as, "he made me mad," consider changing your thought process since you have a choice on how to react to what other people do. You can't change what the other person did, but you can always choose how you will react to it.

Your first 30 days in a new job will no doubt come with a lot of differing emotions. You may find frustration or confusion mixed with enthusiasm and excitement. Your frustration may come off as being impatient or your enthusiasm could be seen as reckless ambition. Having the situational awareness is part of your EQ and soft skills artillery. Knowing how your emotions are affecting your new coworkers could make or break your first 30 days!

Should you be overly critical to how things are being done when you are just starting in your role? Likely not. It is reasonable that you give some time to learn and understand the bigger picture before passing judgment that things should be different.

EQ and Honesty

Being honest is another trait of high EQ and success. Hopefully, your honesty on your resumé, as well as in your interview, helped get you where you are. We all hear that it is best to be honest. Once hired and part of a new team, honesty becomes even more important. While you should always be honest with your employer, you do not have to be an open book and share everything about your life.

Integrity is a broad concept that includes honesty. Some of the important characteristics of integrity include:

1. Being honest. Being honest means speaking the truth. If you call in sick when you're really not, this is not being honest. It disrespects your employer as well as your fellow coworkers. If found out, you lose valuable trust with the team and your employer.

2. Trust and respect. Trust and respect is a type of social currency that can be saved, built up, and used when you need help. Don't spend it foolishly and don't waste it. Being honest earns the trust and respect of others. When you earn the trust and respect of an employee or your team, you gain loyalty.

3. Selflessness. Helping others can go a long way and selfless acts are remembered more than you know. This doesn't mean you allow yourself to be a doormat for everyone to walk all over. However, when you can be helpful, even in small ways such as offering to carry a box for a coworker, or offering to take a customer complaint when a coworker is having a bad day, you can make a positive and substantial impact.

4. Pride and ownership. Taking pride in your work means caring about the quality of the work you produce. Taking ownership means being

committed to doing your part to seeing a project or task through to completion. When you take pride and ownership seeing something through and doing everything you can to ensure a quality outcome, you quickly become a presence that coworkers look up to and your employer can count on.

5. Keeping commitments. When you say you will do something, do it. Integrity means that you can be relied upon. Keeping your commitments plays a big part in that. If you commit to doing something and then back out, you lose integrity and diminish your social currency.

How does having integrity play out in the real-world scenario of employee-employer relationships? Start by thinking about layoffs and promotions. You could be the first in line for a promotion if you are a person of integrity, honesty, and reliability. However, if you are constantly showing you lack integrity by being caught in lies (big or small), producing poor quality work, and not keeping your commitments, you could be the first person on the layoff list.

No employee, job, or company is perfect, and there will certainly be ups and downs. Just know that it's better to approach situations with integrity. Attitude is key and if you come to the table with pride for the quality of your work and a mutual respect, you will get further in any job.

17

Keeping Your Goals in Focus

Sometimes, once we have secured a new job or career, we can lose sight of our goals. We sink into a status quo and focus on what our employer needs today, tomorrow, or next week. Remember in Chapter 1 where you defined your goals and why you want them? It is important to periodically reflect and make sure you continue to achieve your career goals. Remember, it is not your employer's job to advance your career, it is up to you.

Think back, did you accept this job because they offered training, education, upward mobility, or advancement? Have you pursued all of the opportunities offered? How long have you been in your current role? Is it time to change things up to keep you on your career track? Once you have settled in, reflect from time to time, reevaluate, and recommit to your goal!

Write down your career goal? Does it match to what you wrote before?

Have you established and completed the objectives to achieve that goal? Are there new objectives you need to add? If so, what are they?

If you haven't achieved your goal and the steps you have taken already haven't worked, what can you do differently? Is there someone else you know that can help?

If you were hoping to move up in the organization but haven't yet, evaluate how you can best prepare to do so. Consider the following:

1. Mentorship. Connect with a mentor, supervisor, or at least a coworker, that can guide and help with your long-term vision. Mentors can usually be found in organizations at higher levels or perhaps in other departments different from where you currently work. Successful people regularly connect with their mentors. Many mentors are generous with their time, especially when they believe a student is serious and committed to improving. Usually a lunch outside of the work environment is a great opportunity for a mentor and student to be a little more relaxed and candid about opportunities inside and outside the company where they currently work.

2. Cross training. Understanding how your job fits in to the bigger picture is an extremely valuable result of cross training. Consider asking your supervisor if there may be some part time opportunities in a different role within your team, or even upstream or downstream from your department. Many times, while you maintain your current role, you can assist another department just a few hours a day or a few hours a week. Doing this can open your eyes to the value of your current work, allow you to provide feedback to your supervisor and current team about changes that may be impacting your area, and it can sometimes provide perspective on possible next steps for you within an organization.

3. Taking additional classes or training. Did the company offer training that you haven't taken advantage of yet? If not, is there educational reimbursement benefits or seminars that you could find time for? Some universities offer affordable classes online that could help take you to the next level. If your plan included continued training and education, recommit and get to it!

4. Documenting your ideas and achievements. Maintaining a list of the various process improvement ideas, contributions, achievements, or wins in your role makes it much easier to justify your value to your supervisor when the next performance review meeting comes. Don't wait until the day before your meeting to try to think about everything you've done in the past year, you simply won't remember enough of the details to make it seem real. Keep a list and constantly be updating it. Include the date, description, other people involved, result, work hours saved, and financial impact, if any. Definitely include any improvements you have implemented in your job that makes your work more efficient. It is never too early to evaluate your contributions so long as you have made some progressive movement in alignment with the company's vision or mission.

The job honeymoon will likely be over after a year or two, and both you and your employer will continue to evaluate if the relationship is still working. Know that your supervisor or company leadership will likely consider you for other positions within the company as other positions open up. With this in mind, keep track of your performance review timelines and be sure that you are doing all you can to incorporate the company goals and benchmarks into your daily, weekly, monthly, and quarterly activities. Management will emphasize what is important (you can always ask if you're unsure), and getting the job done well by having a positive attitude while achieving the company's goals will be your opportunity to stand out.

18

Performance Reviews

Performance reviews are a formal process to evaluate whether you should keep your current position and possibly earn a raise in pay, transfer to another area, or be considered for advancement or promotion. The key to a successful performance review, just like a new job interview, is your preparation for it. All of the hard work you put into getting the job is now your practice round for your performance review. Sometimes these reviews are formal and systematic, occurring at the end of each quarter or year. Some companies have no formal process, but regularly check in with employees to discuss how they are doing. Regardless of how formal or informal the process, being prepared is your best bet to have a great review and conversation regarding your future with the company.

If you can, do your research ahead of time. Ask other employees about the process, ask your supervisor if there is a form or how items are measured. When the time comes, be ready to have a dialog, both good and bad, without being too defensive. Think of your performance review as an opportunity to review your strengths, achievements, weaknesses, failures, abilities, potential, and goals for the next period.

There are a few different types of systems and reviews that managers and HR departments use. It is extremely helpful if you understand the type of system or review you will be participating in so you aren't completely caught off guard.

1. One-on-One.

   A one-on-one review can go by many different names, but in general, is a formal meeting between you and your direct supervisor. While on any given day, a supervisor may want an informal check-in to talk about a specific issue that occurred recently, a one-on-one is usually more formal and planned in advance. Your supervisor may bring up a list of your accomplishments and where they see you heading as well as pay increases or bonuses company leadership is discussing or planning. They will usually ask how you are doing, what you are struggling with, and how you think you are progressing with your goals. As a planned one-on-one is a formal process, it would be wise to prepare for it just like any other review. Especially if you have the intention to ask for a pay increase or promotion. Sometimes a one-on-one review can be more frequent, such as weekly, monthly or quarterly. On top of this, it is always good to be prepared for an unplanned one-on-one. These can easily arise after a major mistake is made and the supervisor needs to ensure appropriate changes can be made quickly to prevent it from happening again.

2. Rating Scale.

   A rating scale review process is similar to a grading scale used in education. Management will have predetermined outputs they are grading against, and employees with be rated on a grading scale based on the quality of their output. The scale could be 1 to 5, 1 to 10, 1 to 100, or an educational scale like A, B, C, D, F. These scales are commonly used in customer based surveys when they are seeking feedback such as, "Please rate the friendliness of your sales associate on a scale from 1 to 5 with 5 being the best."

3. Self Assessment.

   A self assessment is also another popular employee evaluation. Interestingly, these types of evaluations can sometimes go strongly one way or the other. An employee is either overconfident and believes they are the best employee in the entire company, or they are timid, unsure of themselves, and uncomfortable taking any credit for their rightful accomplishments. Of course, the direct supervisor or manager often knows the real story, but on paper, the HR department may not be able to easily identify that reality. The benefit of a self assessment is the fact that it allows the employee to reflect. It gives them a voice to share their perspective. It also allows an employee and manager to discuss how the manager can better coach or guide the employee in the position to reach appropriate targets. With this type of review, take the time to gather your thoughts and reflect on your positive contributions as well as what you can do to be even better. Then, make a list and be prepared to talk about your results and accomplishments.

4. Employee Participatory System.

   In an employee participatory system, at the beginning of a rating period, the employee will sit down with a manager and determine benchmarks they will meet to measure their performance. The employee and manager will set goals and lay out the actions needed to accomplish those goals. Example goals could be related to production, high customer satisfaction, sales volume, or some other measure. The benefit to this type of system is that if it is set up properly at the beginning of the rating period, and the employee has buy-in that what is measured is a good indicator of whether goals are achieved or not, the employee and supervisor will have an objective way to fairly assess and agree upon the overall performance. However, a challenge of this system can be when employees are measured on different criteria from coworkers with similar positions. The fairness of the criteria is then sometimes called into question.

5. Multiple Feedback.

   Some review systems utilize the perspectives and feedback of managers, coworkers, direct reports and perhaps even customers to grade performance. This review considers feedback and information regarding your performance from almost everyone you may come into contact with. It is meant to provide a well-rounded and balanced view, especially in positions where you have less regular direct contact with your supervisor. The process usually starts with a survey sent to your coworkers, supervisor, manager, customers and direct reports. Scores are tallied by group and you are given a summary highlighting the key points in the survey feedback. The results are then discussed and a plan prepared on how your performance in the next period could improve. With this type of review, it assumes that all of the parties providing feedback are fair and unselfish. This goal may not be realistic for all, especially as some coworkers can be overly critical when evaluating their peers. A big drawback of this type of review is that the process of obtaining all of the survey feedback can be very time consuming for everyone in the organization. If your company is using multiple feedback, keep in mind that you might be restricted in being able to review some of the responses about you that is received. If you are able to review some of the feedback, it is good to try to respond to any negative feedback with any appropriate counter arguments to help put things in a fair perspective about your performance.

Understanding Expectations

No matter the version of review process used, there are things to consider when preparing for a performance review. The most critical is to be sure you understand the expectations, timeline, and process being used. If you're not sure, it is important to ask your supervisor as early as possible. For example, if a rating scale is used, be sure you understand where acceptable benchmarks are. If you think that a 6 out of 10 is okay, it might come as a shock when management expected you to rate above a 7 to be considered on target.

Keep in mind that for companies, it is generally less expensive to keep current employees than it is to hire and train new ones. If your company isn't speaking of layoffs or cost cutting measures and you were hoping for a promotion or raise, then build up your support and then ask! Remember to stay confident, but humble. Performance reviews are a great way for a manager to evaluate your performance, but they are also a great way to evaluate if they are delivering on what they promised in your offer.

Consider the performance review as a positive exercise to reflect and become more aware. You should avoid pointing fingers, shifting blame, or having a negative attitude. This is an opportunity to be a solutions provider. You have a chance to adjust what isn't working and celebrate what is. It's all about attitude and how you approach the matter. Keep in mind that your performance review is a great tool to advance your career.

Here are some items to consider for your review:

1. Job duties. What were the job duties listed when hired? Have they changed? How did you carry out these duties? Did you improve on any duties or were you able to eliminate any unnecessary tasks? Did you take on additional job duties?
2. Your goals. What were your goals for the first 90 days and beyond? Where there any specific performance goals? Learning or advancement goals? Personal Goals? What actions did you take toward your goals?
3. Your accomplishments. Bring your list of ideas and achievements that you have been keeping track of. Did you save time or money on a project? Did you complete a project ahead of schedule? Did you develop a new process or system that was helpful? Your list should capture the details to remember who helped and how impactful it was.
4. Prepare for feedback. You might not agree with the feedback you are given. Keep emotions in check. If feedback is negative, ask how management can support you in your improvement. Offer to take steps for improvement, make suggestions on what you need.
5. Plan your request. Are you wanting to ask for a raise? Are you wanting additional training? A promotion or more responsibilities? Are you looking for additional time off?
6. Future targets. What are your company's new goals for you? What are

the new goals for the company? Are there any concerns or issues on the horizon?

All of the above items will also depend on the frequency of the review process. It is not good practice to continue to meet with your supervisor every month to ask for a promotion or try to renegotiate your pay. Be patient, and be prepared to make your discussion impactful yet reasonable given the frequency of the company's review cycle.

Frequency of Reviews Matters

How frequently a company reviews their employees will matter because this will dictate how you align your performance goals. If the company does quarterly reviews, your 90 Day Plan is more relevant than if they only do an annual review. Remember that whether it is monthly, quarterly, or annually, performance reviews should be treated like interviews! All the previous chapters apply. Being prepared, doing your research, practicing your manners, fine tuning your delivery are all still as important as they were before you were hired. Don't take for granted that your HR department or supervisor fully recognizes all that you have done. Tell an honest story showcasing your contributions, provide supporting details when necessary, and give them a compelling reason to consider you an invaluable member of the company's team. Doing this will provide your best chance to support your career goals in your current position or the next.

19

Ideas to Advance Your Career

There are several ways to go about advancing your career and it all starts with a vision of your long-term goal. If you went through the interview, offer and acceptance process with the company you currently work for, chances are that part of your consideration for accepting the job was potential for advancement.

Advancement can look different or mean different things to different people. If you are just starting your career, the job you currently have could be just a stepping stone to gaining experience and skills which will help you move on to a better position or another organization. If you are mid-career, maybe upward mobility or opportunities to move to another division out of state or country was part of the excitement to accept the offer. If you are more advanced in your career, perhaps you were looking for a longer term position with work-life balance and excellent healthcare benefits. Regardless of what phase you are in your career, your current position is the best place to start when considering your advancement opportunities. Regular performance reviews are the best place to negotiate better pay, position advancement, or benefits. Let's discuss those in more detail.

Leverage Your Review

When you were hired, there is a great chance that you were told about regularly scheduled pay increases that would be attached to performance or perhaps cost of living. You may have also been told that regular reviews would assess your performance, skills and abilities for advancement.

If you planned ahead, such as by preparing a 90 Day Plan, you should already have some strong talking points of objectives completed and goals accomplished. The 90 Day Plan should be reassessed every quarter. That way, you have a well thought out and documented argument to support your case regarding a pay raise or promotion. A 90 Day Plan for each quarter can build on the last to create a compelling story showcasing the best moments of the past year.

The notion that preparation and planning yields better results frequently rings true. The effort that you put into preparing for your job hunt, interview and negotiating your pay and position is the same type of effort you should give when looking to advance.

Keep Your Eyes Open

Just a few generations ago, our great grandparents would get a job and stay with the same company for forty or fifty years and then retire with a good company pension. Those days are gone. Employment with one company for that long is now the rare exception and not the norm. This isn't to say that employees seeking higher pay in the market are solely to blame for this shift. To the contrary, companies are becoming more loyal to shareholder profit than employee retention. Unfortunately, because payroll is one of a company's largest expenditures, sometimes employees are seen as an expense instead of an asset. Throughout the 1980's and 1990's, corporations began phasing out offering company funded pensions and offering 401(k) plans instead. This change essentially put the responsibility of retirement savings in the employee's hands. Bringing this up isn't meant to sour your thoughts on the idea of working for the same company for a long time. Rather, it is to reiterate that you are responsible for your career, and ultimately your retirement, it is not up to the company you work for.

No matter how much you enjoy your current position, or the various exciting opportunities at your current employer, be sure to keep your head up and mind open to opportunities in other organizations. It is very possible that you are one re-organization away from being placed in a different position not suited to your career goals, or even worse, you could be surprised in a layoff as part of a corporate wide reduction in force.

By keeping an eye out for other opportunities, you could improve your negotiating power when your performance review comes up. Monitor industry pay standards and benefits. If you have this information ready to support your case for a raise, you might just be rewarded.

Of course, there are other ways to advance, and sometimes a company with high employee turnover can be a bigger opportunity if you can be patient and ride through the drama.

Advancement

Some of the ways that advancement can happen often have nothing to do with your strategic planning. Sometimes an opportunity comes up and you are the best person who can fill in immediately. Take for instance employee attrition. Employee attrition is when employees leave a company by resignation, firing, layoff, illness, or death. Basically any way, voluntary or involuntary, that employees leave their current position. The other way advancement in an organization can happen is due to an increase in available positions created by company growth. These new positions can be exciting, but sometimes they can be difficult to navigate since there are fewer reference points to know how to best do the job.

Workplaces that have high turnover through attrition can be high stress or high drama and typically include companies such as Information Technology (IT), government, education, food service, sales, and retail. If you work in an industry with high turnover, the chances are very good that if you just stick it out, you will continue to advance as positions are vacated. This is not to say that this is always the best method for advancement. There are other things that can be done.

The Little Things

Pay attention to the little things. Small actions can lead to getting noticed, promoted or getting a raise. Some quick tips:

1. Do what you say you will do. Keeping your word and being reliable builds trust. If you can be counted on, you will be given more responsibility.
2. Avoid drama, gossip and office politics. The best leaders are respected by their peers and direct reports. If you want to be promoted, it is critical that you can be trusted. If you are frequently negative or commonly share in rumors, you may soon be considered untrustworthy. This is because if you talk negatively about others, people will begin to wonder what you say about them behind their back.
3. Be a problem solver. It is always easy for people to complain and point out issues. It is much more difficult to keep focus on problems and what can be done about them. If you can become known as a problem solver, you will be noticed and praised by leadership.
4. Make your boss look good. If you make your supervisor's job easier or make them look good, you will have an advocate when you need it.
5. Take pride in your work. Be committed and do exceptional work. It will be noticed. If you agree to start a project, take it to completion with quality throughout.

If you have done everything you can right, and are told that a raise or advancement isn't in your near future, you may need to reassess where you are and where you are going. Don't feel defeated. Sometimes it happens to the best of us. We get hired, work hard, and sometimes feel like we will remain a hamster running on the same wheel forever. Unfortunately, the reality is that company leaders and managers can't always forecast future company growth precisely, and as a result, work opportunities within their organizations aren't always as originally anticipated.

When Things Aren't What You Expected

If you find yourself in the position where promises were made and not delivered or perhaps the job just isn't what you thought it would be, don't spin on the hamster wheel for too long. A year can easily turn to two and then five. But before you surprise your supervisor by dropping off your letter of resignation, it might be worth a last-ditch effort to try to schedule a meeting to discuss your next steps with calm and thoughtfulness. Things to consider:

1. Talk to your supervisor or a higher level manager about your issues or dissatisfaction. Perhaps your supervisor is fighting for you behind the scenes and you just don't know it. Maybe you can ask for changes in duties or training opportunities to help you advance. If you are a good employee, often your supervisor will find ways to improve your situation because they usually want their employees to succeed. Many times they would rather see you advance to another department and division than see you leave the company.

2. Start your job hunting before you leave. Send out resumés. It is always easier to get a job when you already have one. It will still be serious effort, but prospective employers will not consider you desperate. This means you can normally negotiate a salary at least equal to, if not higher, than your current job. Therefore, it's better not to quit until you have another offer in hand. If you really prefer your current company, and you do get an offer from an outside company, always take it to your supervisor and see if they are willing to at least match it. If they can't or won't, they will not hold it against you that you left the company for a higher paying position, since they would likely do the same.

3. Be cautious. The grass isn't always greener on the other side. If you feel you were misled with your current position, keep in mind that it could happen again. Let your mistakes and experience guide you as you wisely consider the next company's offer.

4. Reconnect. If you have lost touch with your network, reconnect. You should start discretely dipping your toe in the water and getting a feel for

what companies are hiring and what types of positions are in demand.

5. Be discreet. Nothing is more awkward than your boss getting a call for a job reference if they weren't expecting it. If you start sending resumés out and taking interviews, be sure to tell the recipients that you are still employed and would appreciate discretion with your current employer. It is also good to at least quickly mention to your supervisor or your listed references that you are looking at opportunities so they can hear it from you first.

6. Be courteous and professional. Be sure that if or when you accept another job, you ask for the courtesy to give your current employer sufficient notice. Most employers will expect two weeks. Immediately be honest with your current employer. Offer to give them some time to find a replacement and help with a transition.

7. Be ready. With many positions, especially positions with access to sensitive systems or data, don't be surprised if, as you provide your resignation notice, that your supervisor immediately informs you that today will be your last work day. This may especially be the case if you are going to a competing company. Company HR or security professionals may come to assist you in gathering your personal desk items, obtaining your ID badge, and escorting you out of the building. If this happens, don't think you are a bad person. Understand that some companies simply have a policy to have an employee end all their work when notice is given. These companies simply don't want to take a risk that individuals already planning to leave will take property, customer lists, sensitive corporate data files, or under the worst case scenarios, try to sabotage sensitive systems in response to their frustration with the organization.

Keep in mind that career advancement can sometimes happen by baby steps and sometimes by leaps and bounds. Much of it depends on your goals, where you are in your career, your tolerance for change, your awareness to see and assess opportunities that arise, and sometimes a little bit of luck. People are known to change jobs more frequently earlier in their career, sometimes every two to four years on the average. This can be for a variety of reasons such as higher pay, career advancement, or changes in the industry. The IT industry has extremely high mobility rates. Since many tech jobs are in high demand, it only makes sense that companies are continuously competing for top talent.

No matter your pace, your experience, or your industry, hopefully you have gained some additional insight and information that will help you on your career journey.

Parting Thoughts

Enthusiasm and action make great things happen. While not glamorous, job hunting and interviewing is best when approached positively and diligently. Remember that finding a job is a skill in itself and the more you practice in your career, the better you will get. Persistence pays.

Remember to start with your goals. Why are you making a move? What do you want to accomplish? Reflect internally. Do your research on companies you are considering. Do they have a culture that matches your work ethic? Can they help you achieve your career goal?

Consider education and learning as a lifelong process. If a degree isn't required, consider getting certified in something that relates to your field of interest. Companies upgrade systems and change processes all of the time, so even if you are aren't considering continuing education now, it will likely need to be considered in the future.

Remember that job hunting requires preparation to be successful. From resumés and cover letters to manners and attitude, preparation is key. The more you prepare, the more you research, the more knowledge you acquire, the better your chances of rising above the crowd.

Whether interviewing, trying to fit in, or considering your next move for advancement, your attitude and network can lift you up. Always consider anyone and everyone you meet as your next potential employer. Keep in mind that it is a small world and who you interact with may at some point play a role in your next job choice, interview, or offer.

Stay humble, work hard, and walk through your career and life with integrity. While it may feel overwhelming at first to plan and prepare your future, you have tremendous value and you are worth it.

Resources

If you need additional resources to help with a career or job change, there are many local, state, federal and online resources that are free. Below is a list to help get you started:

1. Online job search platforms.
   There are many sites that offer job listings as well as job training and preparation articles, videos, and tools. Here are a few to consider:
   a. Indeed.com
   b. Monster.com
   c. GlassDoor.com
2. Your network.
   Remember that social media, church, friends, neighbors, and schools often are the best resources for job hunting and interviewing.
3. Your college alumni center or career services center.
4. Local or state career centers and employment offices. These are often tied to your state labor and employment offices.
5. Local employment agencies. Some offer not only job placement, but help with resumés, cover letters, and interview preparation.
6. Federal Bureau of Labor and Statistics. They can help research average pay ranges for jobs as well as job projections. You can find the free Occupational Outlook Handbook here https://www.bls.gov/ooh/

Please Rate and Review

If you have enjoyed this book, please rate your purchase on Amazon.com, or your purchase site, to help us reach others. Any remarks or suggestions are highly valued as we continuously strive to make improvements to this and other works. Your feedback on any of the tips or suggestions in this book that you found especially helpful would be very much appreciated!

You can also email any remarks or suggestions for improvement directly to the author at RyanWilmax@gmail.com.

Thank you!

About the Author

Ryan has a diverse professional business background spanning 25+ years in financial, consulting, management, and senior leadership roles while working in a variety of industries including consulting, information technology, manufacturing, government, and real estate. With over 10 years as a manager of financial professionals, Ryan has been responsible for reviewing resumes, interviewing candidates, hiring, and managing effective teams. Ryan received a Bachelor of Science degree in Accountancy, a Master of Science degree in Information Management and has obtained numerous professional certifications. Ryan and his wife enjoy traveling and have taken their twin daughters to all 50 States.

Find out more about Ryan at www.RyanWilmax.com

www.ingramcontent.com/pod-product-compliance
Lightning Source LLC
Chambersburg PA
CBHW071808090426
42737CB00012B/1997